Running your own Business

Made Easy™

Roy Hedges

Running Your Own Business Made Easy
by Roy Hedges

First edition 1999
Second edition 2002
Third edition 2006
   Reprinted 2007
   Reprinted 2008

Lawpack Publishing Limited
76–89 Alscot Road
London SE1 3AW

www.lawpack.co.uk

ISBN: 978-1-905261-05-5

Extracts in chapter 5 relating to discipline and grievance procedures have been reproduced by kind permission of ACAS.

Exclusion of Liability and Disclaimer

For convenience (and for no other reason) 'him', 'he' and 'his' have been used throughout and should be read to include 'her', 'she' and 'her'.

Contents

About the author

Roy Hedges is a freelance writer, entrepreneur and consultant. His practical business guides draw on extensive hands-on experience of starting up, buying and selling businesses himself, ranging from retail grocery outlets to garages and property. His career as an entrepreneur peaked when a firm of bankers' agents that he started grew into a finance company with seven branches, offering trade and consumer finance facilities, before becoming a bank. From this subsidiary, insurance, property and leasing companies emerged. Later, he was to become one of the founding directors of London Trust Securities and Equilease Commercial Finance Ltd. More recently, Roy has been a director of a leading management consultancy and a board member of the leasing subsidiary of a major trade financier and invoice discounter.

Besides addressing manufacturing and trade association gatherings and small business forums on various business topics, he lectures in business studies at Havering College of Further Education and has broadcast on BBC Radio Essex.

Introduction

You have a dream

Sometimes the desire to become self-employed or start a business just isn't enough. Certainly it will give you many new and exciting adventures, but it will also mean that you can no longer rely on others to make decisions for you or lead the way. True, you will take charge of your own destiny, but being in charge also means facing up to the responsibilities that come with being your own boss. Not anyone can run a successful business. It needs commitment, self-reliance and determination.

It can be very lonely making decisions. Any mistake and the buck stops with you. The way you live and work will alter, which at the beginning may not be for the better. The initial 12 to 18 months of any business are crucial. You can expect to work longer hours for less pay and experience feelings of insecurity and isolation. Nevertheless, if you have the right characteristics, a good idea, the capability to plan ahead, and the persistence to overcome any setbacks, then having your own business can be extremely rewarding.

There has never been a better time to start up a business than today, even though the business environment is constantly changing and throwing up fresh challenges. Today's entrepreneurs are better informed, have more help available to them and with the lowest interest for decades, money should no longer be a problem.

The key to success in business is you. Knowing your personal strengths and vulnerabilities will allow you to combat any lack of experience you may have. Learning vital new skills will build self-confidence before you venture into the alien environment of self-employment. Setting up your own business isn't just about setting up a stall, hoping that customers will flock to buy your wares. There is much to learn and do before that day dawns. Fortunately, you will not be alone; you will have help every step of the way.

Roy Hedges

CHAPTER 1

Is running a business for you?

What you'll find in this chapter

✔ Self-assessment questionnaire
✔ Personal objectives and assessing risk
✔ Seeking a business idea
✔ If your business is specialised
✔ Putting down the right foundations
✔ Turning dreams into realities

Running your own business or becoming self-employed can bring rewards and stimulating challenges that working for somebody else never will – if you have the right frame of mind. But knowing where to start can be so confusing. Therefore, the best place to start is with yourself. Do you constantly say to yourself:

- I want my own business but I'm not sure if I've got what it takes.

- I know I could run this firm better than my boss.

- I'm in a dead-end job. How can I take control of my life?

- Can I get a business idea that will work?

If you answered yes to any of these, then perhaps you should be taking the first steps towards forming your own business. But first, take the time to discover if you have what it takes to make your business work.

Going into business with the wrong temperament can be very costly and disappointing. Doing your own thing isn't for everyone. There are no guarantees for success. However, if you have only some of the qualities or skills required, all is not lost. You can change, learn new skills and prosper. Running a business is about putting yourself into other people's shoes and predicting their requirements. Knowledge such as this can be acquired. The following list highlights a few of the most essential characteristics required:

- **Self-starter.** You must be able to identify business opportunities as they arise and confidently act upon them without assistance from others.

- **Determination.** It will take all the determination you can marshal to get your business off the ground.

- **Self-discipline.** Working on your own, sometimes outside normal working hours, will require a high level of self-sufficiency.

- **Accountability.** Blaming others if things go wrong is not possible. The responsibility of being in charge of your business must be enjoyed, not feared.

- **Innovation.** You will need to come up with better methods of operating and new ideas to give your customers the service they deserve on a continual basis.

- **Enthusiasm.** Being enthusiastic about your plans and products gets others involved. It also keeps customers and bank managers on your side.

There are lots of people running flourishing businesses who have neither qualifications nor training. They might lack some of the above traits, but they wouldn't have succeeded without commitment, willpower, a competitive streak and the ability to work extremely long hours. The chances of succeeding diminish quickly unless you can find these things inside yourself. Use the following self-assessment questionnaire to discover to what degree you possess these needed traits. Be honest with yourself when answering the questions. Nothing is gained by being untruthful. The only person you hurt is yourself.

Read each question or statement carefully. Reflect on how strongly you either agree or disagree with it. Show how you identify with each remark by scoring from 1 to 10 at the end of each statement. For example, 1 will indicate you disagree with the question. On the other hand, 10 will signify that you strongly agree, i.e. it sums up your character precisely.

In respect of the question Do I perform well under pressure?, if you concur that you do perform well when under pressure, enter 10. If you feel your work deteriorates under pressure, enter 1. If you believe working under pressure makes you feel uncomfortable, but your work doesn't suffer, enter 4., etc., etc.

Self-assessment questionnaire

		Your score out of 10
1.	Do I perform well under pressure?	_____
2.	Do I stay calm and not get stressed?	_____
3.	I resent influences over which I have no control, affecting my life.	_____
4.	Can I work with and lead a team?	_____
5.	I don't like starting something I am unable to complete.	_____
6.	Does making decisions come easily?	_____
7.	Are the decisions I make usually the right ones?	_____
8.	Am I positive and do I enjoy taking risks?	_____
9.	Am I happier when I don't have to rely on other people?	_____
10.	Do I work well using my own initiative?	_____
11.	Do I bounce back from setbacks and work at a problem until it's solved?	_____
12.	Does the thought of learning new skills and the responsibility of being my own boss excite me?	_____
13.	Do I have the ability to change my mind when it's obvious that an earlier decision was wrong?	_____

14. Does explaining things to others come easy, and am I ever misunderstood? _____

15. Would my partner or I object to business interfering with our private lives? _____

16. Am I a good listener, and can I take advice from others? _____

17. I prefer to stand alone than to be one of a crowd. _____

18. Meeting and dealing with different people is something I enjoy. _____

19. Having my success recognised by others is important to me. _____

20. I am at present in good health and rarely get sick. _____

Total: _____

When you have answered all of the questions and statements, total your score. Look below to see how you shape up to becoming an entrepreneur. If in doubt, give your completed assessment questionnaire to a friend or relation you trust. Ask him for a fair appraisal of your abilities. Don't be afraid of criticism. Learning to accept your faults is another trait you'll need in your armoury. Learning to conquer your failings is the bedrock of successful businesses.

Assessment results

Look for the group into which your score falls. In addition, also reconsider any scores which were either extremely high or low; assess how accurate you have been.

180–200 If your score lies in this band, stress and pressure spur you on. You are dedicated and prepared to work hard to achieve your goals. The risk and insecurity of running your own business will motivate rather than worry you. You have every chance of success with the right business idea and sound planning.

140–179 Certain aspects of running your own business may give you problems. The severity of these will depend on your determination to overcome adversity. Concentrate on improving those areas where you didn't have a high score. However, you seem to have the right frame of mind to deal with the day-to-day pressures of running a business. Your business should flourish and you'll probably enjoy the rewards more than those with a higher score.

100–139 If your scores varied wildly, such as a lot of 1s, 2s, 8s and 9s, you must try to improve the lower scores. Otherwise those regions could be the source of severe problems if you are unable to change them. If this score was reached with reasonably consistent scoring, you should have no cause for concern, but you must ensure that you have a good business plan and be prepared to make use of the various training schemes.

60–99 If your responses were born out of uncertainty, contact your local Enterprise Agency for details of training courses. While you may have the ability to run your own business there are strong indications that you will not enjoy it. Not enjoying your business could cause you to give up under the slightest pressure. Think long and hard about whether you really want to run a business. If you still think going into business is for you, make use of the help and training that are readily available.

Under 60 Running your own business will be a strain – one you may not wish to endure for long. Running a business requires confidence, self-reliance and the competence to handle stress and pressure. Without these traits it would be unwise to set up your own business. You should find out about training courses in your local area to develop the skills you lack.

The above assessment results are only a general guide which assumes that the assessment of yourself was frank and truthful. It's not an appraisal of your technical and commercial proficiency, but of your personal attributes which could affect your business. It's basic, and is intended to give only a broad idea of your aptitude. Contact your local Adult Education College, Enterprise Agency or Business Link today for details of courses in your area, since even with the right personality and attitude, some skills instruction may be required.

Personal objectives and assessing risk

There are usually many reasons for becoming self-employed and your aims can have a direct effect on the success or failure of the business, so they should be considered very carefully.

One of the most common reasons for someone wanting to run their own business is the dissatisfaction they feel when working for someone else. Another might be the belief that they can offer a better product or service than is currently available. Whatever it is, it's important for you to establish your objectives and to know what you want out of your business. You will find it easier to construct your business plan when you are aware of what you expect to gain from the enterprise. Plotting your course carefully will allow you to monitor the progress you and your business are making towards your goals. You'll need the ability to juggle many tasks and the self-assurance to ask questions.

TIP Maximise your strengths by building on your existing knowledge and talents.

Other thoughts that lead people into running their own business include:

- the wish to spend more time with the family;
- the desire to create a new business, help it grow and mature;
- the need to pay off a mortgage in five years;
- the hope of gaining independence;
- the wish to attain a certain level of income (e.g. £100,000 per annum) within a specified timescale.

Did you notice that the motivation behind many of these is the acquisition of money? Being motivated by money alone could mean that you end up spending all your time chasing profits to the exclusion of everything else. While every business needs to be profitable, remember that profits are generated from satisfied customers. Your customers will pay for what they want – not what you wish to provide them. They will not tolerate inferior goods or services. So if you're going into business just for the money, never lose sight of the fact that your customers must always come first.

Managing and assessing risk is an integral part of any successful business, but it's a subject that terrifies many people. Yet we assess and manage risk naturally every day of our lives; for example, when we cross the road. We stand at the kerb assessing the speed of approaching traffic before judging whether it's safe to cross. Doing anything for the first time involves risk of some sort and starting your own business, by its very definition, is an uncertain thing. Using the data gathered in your market research will systematically help you to assess the chances of your business succeeding.

The important part of assessing risk is your ability to implement strategies and tackle tasks that will make your business work. This is why it's important that you're truthful with yourself in the self-assessment questionnaire. This is hard because it's so easy to under- or over-estimate your capabilities. If you have any doubts about yourself, now is the time to do the questionnaire again.

It's impossible to know how you will develop in the long term and react in circumstances you have never previously encountered. Another way of judging whether you can cope is to undertake a SWOT analysis of yourself. In this type of test you simply list the strengths you have and then your weaknesses. Next you list the opportunities available to you and the threats. The idea is to turn your weaknesses into strengths and threats into opportunities. A weakness may be a lack of accounting experience, but you can turn this into a strength by taking a book-keeping course at your local Adult Education Centre or purchase a copy of Lawpack's *Book-Keeping Made Easy*.

SWOT analysis is important to every part of your business including staff, marketing and many other functions, so this matter will be dealt with more fully in later chapters.

Seeking a business idea

Some people want to go into business for themselves but are undecided on the type of business they want to conduct. They may have more than one business idea, or they might wish to consider other options before reaching a decision. Perhaps they are simply seeking a new idea in order to expand an existing business. Whatever business idea you decide upon, it must be something you enjoy doing or are comfortable with.

Business ideas have many origins but they should never be taken in isolation. Many ideas can complement each other to form a final business idea. Potential sources are:

- **Hobbies and interests.** There have been lots of successful businesses born out of a hobby or pastime. You do need to check that your hobby can be turned into a viable business proposition. Remember that while it's easy to get carried away with something you really take pleasure from, not everyone will share your enthusiasm.

- **Personal experience and training** are good sources of inspiration. Experience gained working for somebody else can lead to profitable ideas, as well as professional or vocational training. Do check out opportunities on your doorstep, such as the industry you are currently working in. This will give you added advantages because when you start up your business customers will already know you, thereby creating an instant rapport. This will help you to get your new enterprise off to a flying start.

- **Copying or spin-off products.** This doesn't mean plagiarising someone's patent, design or ownership rights. If you come across a product not available in your area, it may be a good idea to introduce it locally. You may also come across a product or service that with a few changes could meet an alternative market. However, you must get permission from the creator of the product or service. Be careful not to infringe on any registered designs or patents and do take legal advice. It's far better to run a business you have been trained in than to enter a field that is unknown to you.

- **Existing businesses or franchises.** You may wish to take over an established business or purchase into a franchise operation. This option provides an instant business, but will not necessarily remove the risks. A franchiser will have a direct interest in ensuring your success and will work with you in order to get you established, which could include helping to find suitable premises and training.

- **Inventions,** which you have developed, can give you an edge in business. It's advisable to protect your invention by applying for a patent and registering the design. The UK Intellectual Property Office can be contacted for further information by calling 0845 950 0505 (calls are charged at local rate for UK callers only) or via the website at www.ipo.gov.uk. However, protecting your creation can be a complex and costly exercise so do make sure that you get sound advice from your solicitor or accountant.

If your business is specialised

Once you have settled on the type of business you will operate – one that is just right for you – it's now time to get your first taste of red tape. As well as the accepted regulations which all businesses must comply with, there are many businesses from childminders and coffee bar owners to haulage contractors that are affected by specific regulations and will therefore require special licences before they can begin to trade, for example:

- **Entertainment.** All establishments selling alcohol (and this includes pubs, restaurants, hotels, clubs, supermarkets and off-licences) need to apply to their local authority for a licence. This also includes theatres, cinemas, take-aways and community halls. Take care because some individuals supplying alcohol may also need a personal licence. Licensing fees will vary depending on the rateable value of the premises being used. So if your business is connected with entertainment, sport and leisure activities, then check out www.culture.gov.uk/alcohol_and_entertainment for more information.

- **Catering establishments.** If it's your intention to run a business that will make, prepare, handle or sell food, you will need to comply with the hygiene rules to make sure that it's safe to eat. Catering businesses (and that includes those mentioned previously) must register their premises at least 28 days prior to opening. Some businesses, butchers for example, must be approved and licensed before trading starts. Those businesses that will sell pre-packed food to other food businesses or consumers must include specific information about the contents on the packaging. To find out more about food hygiene and safety regulations, go to www.food.gov.uk.

- **Health and care services.** Childminders, care homes and other businesses looking after people must register with the relevant governing body. Childminders, nurseries, out-of-school clubs and pre-schools must register with the Office for Standards in Education (Ofsted). This also includes all education establishments, such as boarding schools. On the other hand, care homes, home care and nursing agencies must register with the Commission of Social Care. Providers of independent medical care, including laser treatments, need to register with the Healthcare Commission, while massage services and businesses that pierce skin, such as tattoo artists, are required to be licensed by their local authority's environment health department. To contact any of the above government agencies for further details, see their respective websites at www.ofsted.gov.uk, www.csci.org.uk and www.healthcarecommission.org.uk.

- **Transport businesses.** Hauliers using vehicles with a plated weight of more than 3.5 tonnes require an Operator Licence. This applies even if the vehicle has been hired or you are transporting goods just for one day. There are a number of different types of licence and the one you will need will depend on whether you are transporting your own goods or those of other people and if you are transporting the goods within the UK or abroad. Strict rules apply for safety reasons if hazardous materials are being transported.

Those businesses carrying people must also obtain a licence if they are running a taxi or a private hire vehicle (minicab) carrying fewer than nine passengers. These licences can be obtained from a local authority. If you are carrying passengers in a vehicle with more than eight seats, you will normally require a Public Service Vehicle (PSV) Operator Licence. Licences are issued by the local Traffic Area Office. Strict rules governing maintenance, the length of time commercial drivers can drive and the type of licence they must hold apply, so check very carefully as penalties can be severe. Before commencing this type of business you are advised to contact the

Vehicle & Operator Services Agency, which can provide you with details of your local licensing office at www.vosa.gov.uk. For information relating to driving licences, visit www.dvla.gov.uk and the Department for Transport will provide information about drivers' hours, working time rules and how to transport dangerous goods at www.dft.gov.uk.

- **Other specialised businesses.** The above are just a few of the more popular types of businesses which require special requirements before they can operate. There are many other businesses whose activities are regulated and licensed, from manufacturing businesses to street traders, boarding and breeding kennels, as well as money lending. What you must do next is to check if the business you intend setting up is effected by special regulations and you can do this by contacting www.businesslink.gov.uk. Your local authority's environmental health or trading standards can assist with licences, and for credit licences for lending money, debt collection or hire services, check with the Office of Fair Trading at www.oft.gov.uk. A list of all local government websites are available from www.direct.gov.uk.

Some businesses, such as nurseries who drop off and pick up children from their schools, will be required to register with Ofsted, but at the same time could infringe on the transport regulations if they use a vehicle with more than eight seats for this purpose. A nursery owner will also need to check that his vehicle insurance is adequate for this purpose.

Putting down the right foundations

Knowing what you want from life and having the correct skills and attitude means that you can start to lay a strong foundation for the business of your dreams. However, when you are self-employed, you will need to juggle different sorts of tasks. While you cannot be expected to possess the knowledge of an accountant or personnel manager, you will probably have to learn new skills to ensure that you have the rudimentary ingredients of any profitable business.

Training is available, both for those who are already in business and for those who are still in the planning stage. Such training implies spending months in preparation before opening the doors of your business, but the time and effort that you put in will be time well spent.

Some of the skill shortages you may face are:

- **Management.** Whether working alone or with others, you must be able to manage and control your business.

- **Financial.** It's important to know that your business has sufficient funding and cash flow for it to operate. Simple book-keeping knowledge will be sufficient, but don't forget that getting paid on time is crucial!

- **Sales and marketing.** Learning how to keep your customers supplied with what they require and how to make a profit by doing so. There is more information and assistance on this subject further on in the book.

- **Production and transportation.** If you manufacture the products you are selling, you must guarantee your goods meet with your customer's requirements and that the goods are delivered as required. The earlier segment regarding licensing needs to be heeded to avoid any unnecessary problems arising.

You may not need to have an in-depth knowledge of all these subjects, merely a basic understanding, since it's possible to buy these skills in, as and when the demand arises. Knowing which fundamental skills are needed and how to keep your business running profitably can be the basic building block of success.

 Make sure that you understand the implications of setting up a business. Be ready to tackle anything legal to get what and where you want.

Turning dreams into realities

Making sure that you have all the information needed before starting to trade is essential. There are a number of business support agencies just waiting to hear from you, so if you are unsure where to start, look in your local *Yellow Pages* for one of the following:

- Business Links
- Chambers of Commerce
- Small Business Enterprise Agencies
- Adult Education Centres
- Your local council

Never be afraid to ask questions. One of the major causes of business failure is lack of sufficient information. Make certain that you are adequately prepared for what lies ahead.

In a nutshell, being in business means keeping an open mind about new ideas and overcoming any skill shortages you may have through training. Above all, it means that you don't take short cuts but prepare yourself thoroughly. Keep a list of your personal objectives to hand at all times. Never lose touch of your original targets. Accept responsibilities cheerfully and enjoy your business.

 No two business are alike. Whatever type of business you choose, it will have its own set of requirements. The hazards facing someone who proposes working from home, without additional staff, will be completely different from a limited company planning to open a chain of computer game retail outlets.

CHAPTER 2

Will your ideas work?

What you'll find in this chapter

✔ Field research
✔ Interpreting market information
✔ Knowing who your customers are
✔ Pricing your goods or services
✔ Learning about competitors
✔ Finding your market
✔ Using a market research agency
✔ The nuts and bolts of marketing

The best product or service in the world is of little value unless there are people who want to buy what you have to offer. It's therefore essential to have a viable marketing plan before you go into business.

But what is marketing? The Chartered Institute of Marketing describes marketing as 'the process responsible for identifying, anticipating and satisfying customer requirements profitably'.

Marketing comes in two guises – the first being market research. This informs you whether there are a significant number of customers to buy your wares or services and where they can be found. The aim of this chapter is to help you do just that.

The other side of marketing is the art of persuading people that your services and goods are what they need, rather than those of your competitors. We deal with this subject in chapter 3.

Market research is about knowing who and where your competitors are located, the type of goods or services they provide and what they charge. Having this information at your fingertips will help you stay one step ahead of them constantly.

Time and effort spent on reliable market research will be rewarded many times over. Such research not only will tell you who your customers are, but also will provide you with a very clear indication of why they will buy your goods or services. Gathering this information will make your job a lot easier when it comes to selling your products or services. It will also inform you what your potential customers have in common. For example, if the majority of your customers enjoy sailing, it would pay you to advertise in a yachting magazine, or perhaps to set up a stall at one of the boat shows held around the country. Advertising your products in a cycling periodical, however, would be a complete waste of money.

But not all your customers will form into one solid group or have one single interest. When analysing your potential customers it's more than likely that they will fall into 'segments' (i.e. sub-groups). Identifying these sub-groups will let you direct your efforts once your business starts to trade more accurately and make your sales campaigns more effective and cost-efficient.

From your market research you will need to establish a list that will help you assess the segments within your customers, such as:

- what significant type of groupings you have identified;
- the common features shared by the members of each group;
- where your potential customers are situated;
- how you can sell to them;
- the social, legal, political and economic factors affecting the market;
- the strengths and weaknesses of the competition;
- what the market share can achieve;
- what prices should be set, and what terms of trade you should offer.

Once you have completed your list, take a look at the pros and cons of each group to establish if they will contribute to the sustainability of your business. Completing this task will allow you to identify your target market. This, in turn, will demonstrate where you need to direct your sales efforts. It will also assist you to answer the following questions:

- What will be the principal aims of my business?

- What type of goods or services should I be selling?

- What type of customer mix will help maximise profits?

It's important to have a balanced market as this will go a long way to stabilise your business. The right balance for you may rely on the nature of the local market, the different types of potential customers available and, most decisively, who your competitors are targeting.

 A good idea alone will not guarantee you success.

Conducting such research should also provide you with valuable insight into the current state of whichever market you decide upon, and it will answer these two essential questions:

- Is there a market for my product or service?

- Can I get an adequate market share to make my enterprise worthwhile?

 Marketing is about giving your partners what they want, when they want it, and at a price that is worthwhile to both.

Once you have obtained this information, you will need to look further into trends in the marketplace, potential customers, competitors and test marketing. Your should bear in mind that while these sections are inter-related, they will be dealt with individually in this book.

Any market research you conduct must be planned and not done 'ad hoc'. However, before spending a lot of time and effort on your own research, take a look at the published research material that is available to you free of charge.

Much of the information you require can be gained without leaving your home. Your first port of call should be the media. Television, the internet and newspapers – both national and local – give very useful trade data.

Trade magazines are another specialist reservoir of information. In addition, most banks have a business department which should provide valuable facts and figures on industry trends, and Business Links (the Department of Trade and Industry) and small Business Enterprise Agencies will provide you with statistics on both the home and export markets. Don't forget your local Chamber of Commerce, trade association or your local council. Your regional reference library should keep reports created by any of the above bodies. If they don't, they will always point you in the right direction.

 When analysing your findings, take into account any regional or seasonal trends.

Consider the following when examining your findings:

- What is the size of the market locally, nationally or internationally?
- Is the market expanding, contracting or stagnating?
- What is the per cent of change?
- Is the market volatile?
- Is there any legislation, or technical, economic or environmental changes, taking place at the moment that may affect the marketing of your product or service in the future?

Once you have completed your research, write down your findings. They will be needed to construct your business plan, which is demonstrated for you in chapter 8.

Field research

Market information and your own data can tell you a lot about your potential and existing customers, as well as your market, but it's unlikely to tell you everything you need to know.

To supplement the intelligence you have gathered, you will need to conduct your own field research. This will involve you talking, observing or carrying out product testing or, in the case of service industries, providing free tester sessions. This will assist you in:

- testing customers' reactions to new products or services;
- adapting the product or service as necessary;
- investigating the attitudes of both existing and potential customers;
- discovering local information explicit to your business, rather than the market as a whole.

Research of this nature can be either quantitative or qualitative. Quantitative research provides you with statistical information; for example, how many likely customers there are and their average incomes. On the other hand, qualitative research studies customers' feelings and their frame of minds towards your goods or services and what inspires them.

Good planning for a field research project is essential if you want to get the results right. Deciding how you wish to collect the information you want is the first step. There are various methods you can use, such as face-to-face or telephone interviews using a fixed set of questions. Another possibility is the postal survey, which is fine for the large market research firms, but poor responses due to people's laziness don't recommend this for the small fledgling business.

 Market research questionnaires that are short and simple get the best results.

Discussions held in small focused groups are excellent for qualitative research as they allow you to explore people's responses to your products or services in greater detail. Investigating what people do rather than what they say is called 'observation research'. Looking at how shoppers react to a special point-of-sale display as they pass by is one example.

Alternatively, you may wish to blind test your product with that of a competitor. This is used mainly in the food industry. Lending a new product to a few customers and requesting feedback from them is one method of experimenting how your goods will meet your customers' needs. As mentioned above, taster sessions in the service industries really do work, particularly in the childcare sector.

Once you have decided how you will gather the information you require, you will now need to work out how this will happen and what it will cost you in both time and money. The emphasis will probably be on the time element rather than cost. Having budgeted your market research, your other tasks will now concentrate on:

- **Design for your research.** This will include drawing up a questionnaire or choosing how to run your discussion group.

- **Logistics.** Do you want to run a focus group, conduct face-to-face interviews or organise product tests? Where do you want to hold them? Where do you find the participants and who will run the session?

- **Skills.** Do you have the right skills or the time to do either of the above or should you use a market research firm to do it for you?

To help you with your decisions and maximise your effectiveness in conducting a market research campaign, here are some useful tips:

- **Ask the right questions.** Badly-phrased questions can produce misleading answers. Questions that only prompt 'yes' or 'no' answers should be ousted from your questionnaire. A tailor who asks male customers if they will buy a shirt will be told 'yes' or 'no'. Asking the customer if he will buy a short- or long-sleeved shirt, striped or plain with single or double cuffs and size, will give the tailor a better idea of what to or not to stock.

- **Use a logical order.** Your very first question should tell you if the interview is worth continuing. For example, if you are trying to research the market for a new car accessory, your first question should be, 'Do you own or drive a car?'

- **Talk to the right people.** A survey conducted at, for example, a local school will get answers from women with children. If you propose to target single people or those without children, your survey will not be reflective on your actual market.

- **Talk to enough people.** A survey conducted with one or two dozen people will not supply you with sufficient information. Larger numbers, say 150 to 200 people, will provide you with a more complete picture of your chosen market.

- **Make your research impartial.** It's so easy to encourage people to supply you with the answers you want to hear. Smiling at the right answer or asking leading questions are just a couple of examples. Discussions where you don't work from a set list of questions are easy to distort. Take care if you are using a focus group as some individuals with strong views may influence the opinions of others.

Interpreting market information

While there is a lot of marketing information available, care needs to be taken when analysing it. For one thing, it may not be in a format that is easy to use and the range of information may not tally with your target market.

Beware of out-of-date information. The market you propose to enter may have changed since the material was published and it can be difficult to detect how up to date the information is on the internet. Furthermore, the source of the information may be biased.

As for statistics, they can sometimes mask the true picture. Published averages of, say, income could hide a mix of very high and low earners, meaning fewer people are able to afford your products or services. This principle also applies to existing customers where one or two very large customers could distort your reports.

 Don't make your mind up in advance. Finding information that CAUTION matches what you already believe is easy. Only a realistic picture of your potential market is useful to your business.

Take the utmost care when interpreting the results of your survey and make sure the conclusions you draw are the correct ones from your research. Bear in mind that people may distort answers in the hope of getting you to do something, such as lowering the price, simply by answering that they would be interested in your product or service if the price was modified.

Qualitative research that investigates the feelings and attitudes of customers is particularly difficult to interpret.

Do be realistic when analysing the results of your survey. It can be very tempting to pick out the answers that confirm what you want to hear and forget the rest. Ignoring negative results could be very harmful to your business. Once all your market research is completed and the results known, you may find it necessary to amend your original business plans or ideas.

Knowing who your customers are

It will be helpful to construct a customer profile for each product and service you propose to offer. Marketing professionals use the following grades to define social status groups:

Social Grade	Occupational Group
A	Top management, administrative and professional
B	Intermediate managerial
C1	Supervisory, clerical and junior management
C2	Skilled manual workers, pensioners
D	Semi-skilled and unskilled manual workers
E	Unemployed, casual labourers

Classification could also be based on characteristics and common interests shared by your customers.

Other ways to classify groups of customers are:

- Sex, age, ethnic group, marital or parental status
- Education, skills, culture, religious or political beliefs
- Profession, occupation, self-employed, financial
- Geographically, habits, hobbies, height and weight
- Industry, number of employees, turnover exceeding a specific figure
- Special events, marriage, sports or clubs
- Ownership of cars, pets and houses

Customers will come in all shapes and sizes, but they should all have one thing in common: the desire to buy your goods or services.

An average customer profile can be a mixture of classifications. For example, a travel agent specialising in winter sunshine holidays may target people over 60 on the basis of geography, as well as nationally and socially (Grades B and C), and by interest (they may have an interest in walking). A wallpaper manufacturer would target wholesalers and trade outlets instead of individuals. Additionally, the manufacturer might take the financial status or company size (those customers likely to order in excess of £3,000, for instance, in a stated period) into consideration.

Apart from dividing up your customers into quantifiable categories, you will also wish to classify your customers by what they want. Identifying your customers' needs is more likely to bring about the success of your business than anything else. After all, if you don't have any customers, you won't achieve any profits!

So how do you find out what your customers want? Ask them – both the new and existing customers – what they are looking for and then combine this with the information gained from your research in market trends. These answers will provide you with a good idea of what people want and how much they are prepared to pay for it.

Simply knowing if your customers travel to work by public transport or car can be useful to some businesses. One valuable free source of profiling for those businesses selling to the end user is www.checkmyfile.com, which provides a profile report by postcode. Also, your local council's website can provide you with a 'ward profile', which lists the type of properties people live in, their occupations and their ages. This information is listed by electoral wards or by postcode and will provide you with a valuable insight into who is living in your proposed trading area.

Customers are really only interested in what your product or service will do for them – they are looking to fulfil a desire. Examples of customers' needs fall into the following general divisions:

- Product reliability, after-sales service and support
- Right product, right quality, flexibility, delivery and competitive price

- Honesty, fulfilment/satisfaction, pleasing service and environment
- Confidence in your expertise, status, generous terms of trade

Even once you have identified your customers and made sure that your product or service meets their needs, your pricing policy may still dramatically affect sales.

Some people only gather information when they are starting up. Failing to keep track of how markets are developing and what competitors are up to could be disastrous. Don't fall into this trap!

Pricing your goods or services

Pricing is a very delicate matter and, as studies have shown, you must get it right initially. Prices that are too high will cause your customers to go elsewhere. Prices that are too low will make you little or no profit. Undoubtedly, it's a very sensitive area. Most small businesses tend to over-emphasise the importance of price and undercut their competitors. This can lead to bankruptcy or liquidation. Instead, it's wise to compete on factors such as quality or service, before taking the drastic step of cutting prices.

A well-constructed pricing policy not only ensures that you operate your business profitably, but also helps you make the most of your opportunities.

Price is not always the overriding factor. A carpenter targeting Grade B house owners was inundated with work by recommendation because of his honesty. The customers needed to leave the carpenter alone in their homes and needed to trust him implicitly. Due to the manner in which he fulfilled their trust, the actual price of his work in these circumstances wasn't an issue. Honesty, reliability and solid workmanship carried the day.

So what do you need to know when it comes to pricing your goods or services? It's important to work out all your costs as accurately as possible.

These come in two categories: fixed costs, such as rent, lighting, heating, wages and insurance, and variable costs, which can increase or decrease depending upon the level of business activity. Examples of variable costs include bad debts, raw materials, transport, postage and packing.

Watch out for hidden costs, such as wasted stock or materials, depreciation, pilfering and the full costs for providing service.

Don't overlook Value Added Tax (VAT). This is applied to goods and services, and is currently 17.5 per cent, except on household fuel. Your sales must reach a certain threshold before you need to register for VAT. Your local HM Revenue & Customs office will send you the relevant details.

 Check other suppliers for bulk discounts and other offers, such as extended credit.

Learning about competitors

You can locate your competitors from a number of sources. The easiest source is the *Yellow Pages*, but your suppliers might be another, if they're willing to tell you who else they supply. If you're thinking of going into retail, simply walking the streets will identify many of your potential competitors. In addition, local business clubs, Chambers of Commerce, and trade and professional associations can normally help.

One method of finding out about your competitors is to unobtrusively stand outside their premises, taking notes of deliveries, customers, prices and the general level of activity. This sort of surveillance can also supply you with useful information on suppliers or potential customers that you may not have known about. You should make sample observations of each competitor on different days and times.

Try to sample your competitors' products or services and compare them with your own. If this isn't possible, obtain their sales and promotional literature. Try to talk to as many of your competitors' customers as you can. Find out why they buy their goods and services. Remember, anyone offering the same, or similar products and services, is a competitor.

Consider the following points when analysing your competitors:

- What gives you an advantage over your competitors?
- What advantages do your competitors have over you?
- Does your product or service have a unique selling point?

All the information you have collected about your rivals, either individually or as a whole, will be needed when putting your business plan together.

 Finding no obvious competitors doesn't mean that you will have the field to yourself – it may mean that there is no market for your idea.

Finding your market

Aided by the information you have accumulated in your market research, you will now be in a position to put together a marketing plan. This will summarise your research and show, at a glance, how you will market your product or service. Moreover, it will project your expected sales figures. Any prospective investor or lender will expect you to be able to predict future turnover and to clearly demonstrate how this will be achieved.

If you have completed your market research correctly, then your marketing plan should be self-evident. This plan will be in the form of a spreadsheet and will provide a breakdown of:

- Units sold and price
- Targeted market and method of selling
- Value of sales, plus monthly and annual forecasts
- Promotion and advertising costs

You can do this for each product or service you offer, or for the business as a whole. You must be confident that you can deliver the figures stated in your marketing plan. Some of the information in your marketing blueprint will also be used later in your profit and cash flow forecasts.

Now, you might be saying to yourself, 'If I haven't been in business before, how can I be expected to have sales figures from which I make these forecasts?' The answer is test marketing.

Test marketing can be conducted as a supplement to, or instead of, other research. A well-thought-out test marketing plan can provide information on many of the areas mentioned above in the market research section. In particular, take note of the success rate of experimental promotions. Find out which ones worked and why they did so, not forgetting to list those that were less effective. This will maximise results and reduce costs. Test marketing is a minimum cost venture to measure a market response. In other words, a 'toes in the water' exercise whose main objective is to make potential customers aware of your product or service and gauge the general level of interest.

Trial marketing is the one 'sure-fire' way to find out if your ideas will work. It's not necessary to actually trade to conduct a test-market exercise, and it can be done in a number of ways. Forums that will readily assist you in conducting your research are:

- **Advertising.** Place an advert or a series of differently-worded adverts in a suitable media. Advertise the product or service or offer further information to those who respond.

- **Websites.** If you have access to a computer, it's easy to set up a simple website. Most website providers offer free pages with guidelines about how to set up your own web page. Just count how many people visit your site each day and what information they are seeking about your goods or services.

- **Mailshots.** Send details to a sample list of potential customers or clients. If, for example, four out of every 100 buy from you, valuable information has been gained. You have then started to develop a marketing strategy.

- **Leaflet distribution.** The cheapest and easiest to conduct: sample a target group in your area and you will be able to immediately gauge the response.

- **Demonstrations.** Arrange to give demonstrations of your product or service to local groups or clubs. Perhaps a large store will give you space. Trade exhibitions not only are a useful way to test market your products or services, but also will enable you to keep an eye on what your competitors are up to at the same time. The level of interest can be instantly gauged – an added advantage.

Whatever method you use, the end results should be sufficient for you to gauge the potential size of the market and should confirm the feasibility of trading in the market segment tested.

 Having a thorough understanding of the market in which you trade will keep you one step ahead of the competition at all times and assist you to sell your goods or services.

Using a market research agency

Although you may be able to conduct your own field research, it's time-consuming. It therefore may be beneficial and more cost effective to outsource this task to professionals for the following reasons:

- A market research agency may get better results. It has the experience to design questionnaires, run focus groups and ask the right questions.

- Customers may be more relaxed with a professional and find it easier to be more honest with their answers.

- Customers may worry that you could be trying to sell them something when conducting the survey yourself.

- An outsider can be more impartial, particularly if people are criticising your product or service.

The problem with a small or new business using a market research agency is the cost. Most agencies will not take on projects with a budget of around £3,000 or less. However, you could use a freelance researcher.

Use an online directory, such as www.yell.com, to find a market research agency or freelance researcher. Recommendations from business contacts are another option.

Before commissioning an agency or freelancer, do investigate his background. Ask for a list of previous clients and contact them for feedback. Check that the agency or freelancer has the relevant experience and knowledge and consider if you would be comfortable working with him.

If street interviews are to be conducted as part of your strategy, ensure that the researchers fit the image of your business and that they have the required licence from the local authority and will carry an identity card.

Finally, it's imperative that you get a clear idea of what the fees will be for the service you want. Make sure that you provide the agency or freelancer with thorough instructions. This should cover your business objectives behind the project, the information the research should uncover and how you intend to use the results. To avoid any unnecessary disputes, provide your brief in writing and get written confirmation of the costs.

The nuts and bolts of marketing

Market research is the one area in business where 'big is best'. You may not be able to afford the fees of the top consultant firms in this country, but the websites of firms such as PricewaterhouseCoopers, and Ernst and Young carry enough information in the public domain to meet the research needs of the small business. It's sites like these that should always be your first port of call.

Discipline is the order of the day if you are carrying out your own research. Make it part of your routine to carry a notebook, pen and a pair of scissors with you wherever you go. Newspapers sometimes carry useful research data or you may overhear a snippet of information on the tube or train that could be helpful. Writers do this all the time. Actions like these can yield a number of good business ideas and a lot of valuable business information.

- Split your research into three groups: market trends, competitors and potential customers.

- Invest time not money – it's the most vital research commodity.

- Focus your research by drawing up a wish list of three or four dream customers and then think about their needs.

Gathering marketing information should be an ongoing activity. In business, you must always be aware of your main groups of customers and their interests and needs. In addition, you must know the extent to which your products or services go to meet these needs. Above all, continually assess the best methods of getting your goods or services before the customer.

Also, the constant need to know what your competitors are doing can be a matter of survival for your business.

CHAPTER 3

Promoting and selling your wares

What you'll find in this chapter

✔ Getting your business noticed
✔ Designing your firm's image
✔ Getting customers to buy
✔ Terms of trade
✔ Looking after existing customers
✔ Every business needs a customer service agenda
✔ Dealing with customer complaints

Whether you are trying to entice new customers or satisfy existing ones, quality and image count. If the conception you are promoting is appealing, and the product or service you are offering is appreciated, then pulling in and retaining customers shouldn't prove difficult. It's more cost effective to keep existing customers than to have to replace them. Of course, you will still have to remind them from time to time of what you do or sell and what values you stand for, as well as keeping them informed of any new products or services you introduce. This is what advertising is all about!

 Dissatisfied customers usually shout louder than most. It might have taken years to build healthy customer relationships, but it only takes a few minutes for an unhappy customer to undo all your hard work.

Your reputation is a priceless commodity. It takes a long time to acquire it and it can be lost all too quickly. Recommendations made by satisfied customers cost nothing, but they can increase your turnover more quickly and consistently than any expensive advertising campaign.

Creating a good concept about your products and business need not cost you the earth. Answering the telephone in a polite, business-like manner is easy. Printed stationery items including letterheads, invoices and business cards can be produced relatively cheaply these days. Money is usually tight in small businesses, so you must make every penny count. Take every opportunity to ask customers how they heard of you. If possible, keep a record of their replies – this will tell you what advertising has been effective and what has not.

Keeping track of the type of advertising that works and discovering what doesn't requires the use of only a simple form or if you have a computer, a spreadsheet along the following lines:

Type of Media		Date of Publication		
Customer Details	Date of Enquiry	Date Literature Sent	Date of Follow Up	Results

It's advisable to use a separate form for every newspaper or media source you intend using.

Getting your business noticed

Almost every business needs to promote itself in some way. Reaching out to potential and existing customers comes under the general heading of advertising. This builds confidence in new products and services and creates demand.

Before you can sell your products or services you need a potential customer. Some advertisements will promote a particular product or service with the aim of inviting the public to order the product directly by completing an order form included in the advertisement. This encourages readers to telephone or email an order line or visit their local store.

Others, and this applies more to business-to-business sales, use an advertisement with the aim of attracting potential customers to their business and once these potential customers get in touch, they are able to bring in the sales team to get those interested in the product or service to actually buy what is on offer.

There are many ways you can advertise your business and by monitoring the results of each advertisement, you will ensure that you are not wasting your precious financial resources on loss-making advertising. The normal advertising routes are:

- Media – newspapers, magazines, posters, cinemas, radio and television
- Direct approach – using mailshots and/or telephone canvassing
- Internet
- Point of sale

Which one of the above should you choose? The nature of your business may well dictate the best method for you. You may need just one of the above categories or maybe two or more will maximise the impact of your campaign. However, you must use whatever combination you feel is right for your business.

Advertising needs to be constant. Just placing the odd advert now and again can sometimes do more harm than good. A successful advertising campaign must be well thought out and balanced.

 The logic of advertising is to allow firms to reach their fullest potential and grow.

There is one thing common to all forms of promotion, whatever the method used, and it doesn't matter if your intention is to attract new customers or retain old ones, and that is an eye-catching headline.

Newspapers and magazines

There are many newspapers, both local and national, as well as the free ones to choose from. The same goes for magazines, but you must select those best suited to your service or product.

When putting your advertisement together it needs to be like any good story, with:

- a beginning designed to make the reader want to learn more about what you are offering and read on;

- a middle to let him know what the item or service can do for him; and

- an ending that will urge him to rush out or pick up the telephone to buy whatever you are offering.

Your advertisement must be strategically placed, eye-catching and easily understood.

 In advertising you should keep the text simple. Never use words people can't understand without using a dictionary.

Because space is at a premium you need to get your message across using the fewest number of words possible. Your advertisement will be sitting alongside and competing against the news or a short story in a magazine, so it must stand out and be interesting. The wonderful thing about writing advertising copy is that it doesn't need to be grammatically correct; you can write as you speak. Concentrate on the headline, as this is the main thing that will tempt customers to try your product or find out more about your service.

Advertisements that have a visual content are far superior to those with pure prose; otherwise it can be difficult to separate the latter from the normal contents of a newspaper or periodical. This form of advertising falls into two distinct categories and these are:

1. **Direct response.** This type of advertisement invites the reader to do something; for example, to reply to an address or telephone number for further information, such as a brochure or catalogue. It can also include an order form or coupon.

    A point to note when using a reply coupon in your advertisements is that you must place it in a position where it can be cut out easily (e.g. the top or bottom of a page on the outside edge is ideal). Try cutting out a coupon from the centre of a newspaper to see what I mean. Front and back pages are preferable to inside the paper, but this comes at a cost.

2. **Indirect response.** This type of advertisement draws the reader's attention to a product range (e.g. a certain make of car). Its aim is to get you to call into a shop or showroom to purchase the item at a later date. Posters also fall into this category.

The aim of all advertising must be to:

- generate awareness of your product or service;
- reverse the efforts of competitors;
- get customers to respond;
- improve reliance on your products or services;
- compile a mailing list.

When purchasing advertising space, you get what you pay for. If newspapers or magazines offer you large discounts at a specific time of the year, it usually means that fewer readers will be seeing your advertisement. Selecting the position for your advertisement is as important as the content; never leave it to an editor to place your advertisement as he will place it in any empty space convenient for him.

 When designing your advertisements make sure that your contact details (e.g. name, address and telephone number) are prominently displayed.

When opening a magazine or newspaper, the right-hand pages are usually noticed first and a page with more news content than pictures will make your advertisement stand out from the crowd, especially if it has some form of visual content. To give you an example of the importance of placing the advertisement in the right place, a sportswear manufacturer will insist on his advertising being placed within the sports section of a newspaper to maximise impact. On the other hand, if that same manufacturer was advertising in a sports magazine, the exact position may not be as relevant.

Radio and TV advertising

Unlike newspaper advertising, which is sold by the amount of space it takes up, radio and television adverts are sold in slots of ten-second segments. At one time, radio and television advertising was solely the domain of the very large corporations. Now, with the advent of local radio and regional television, this form of advertising is available to all. At certain times during the course of the day the cost of some TV slots come within the reach of the smaller business. If you are offering the right product or service to fill those slots, it's a media worth considering.

 Keep music and special effects to a minimum as they can distract the listener or viewer from your message.

An important point to bear in mind when scripting a commercial is to leave 20 to 25 seconds for ordering or contact details out of a 60-second slot. Repeat your firm's name, contact address and telephone number at least twice. Keep the address simple by using a post office box number rather than a lengthy address. With this type of advertising the timing of every syllable, sound effect or note of music is crucial to get the right message across to the listener or viewer within a reasonable timescale.

We write and talk at different speeds, so the advertisement must be accurately timed. When you have written your script read it out loud and time yourself from beginning to end to ensure that it's right. After you have read it through, each time rewrite the script as necessary until it matches the slot you have purchased.

Costs for an actor to record voice-overs could easily eat into your profits needlessly. As commercials are recorded, you can easily do them yourself. All you need is a little practice and you will be confident enough. Don't try to mimic an actor or announcer as it will sound false – just be you. If you 'um' and 'aah' a little, don't worry as the message will come across more naturally. When recording, keep a picture of your best friend in your mind's eye, and talk to him. As with the sales letter, think of yourself as addressing one person and not a large audience.

The major advantage of television over other media is that you can demonstrate your products' unique selling points. Use simple everyday language to get your sales message across to the buying public. At the end of every commercial invite the audience to do something, such as pick up the telephone and request a brochure or order your product right away. To get the listener or viewer to act **now** offer them some form of incentive; for example, a double glazing firm could offer a free front door to anyone ordering five or more new windows within 48 hours. Incentives alone are never enough for a good advertising campaign. Always stress the benefits your product or service will give the buyer and remember its unique selling points.

 Advertising slots either very late at night or early morning can be cost effective. Not everyone sleeps at the same time as you.

Using this type of media, one-off commercials seldom work. Be prepared to book a small series of slots as repetition really does work. If a potential customer missed getting your contact details written down with the first advertisement, he will be ready at the next one. People buy from firms they can trust and know and with reiteration they will feel that you will be there tomorrow. In addition, booking a series also lets you negotiate on price.

The type of programme in which you advertise can make or break a campaign. Use talk shows instead of music programmes. The talk show listener is tuned into the voice and will not be put off by your advertisement. Avoid rush hour periods as those travelling by public transport will not hear your message, and those driving will not be able to write down your contact details.

Your unique selling point

Before we go any further, let's talk about USPs. USP stands for 'unique selling point' (i.e. the thing or things which distinguish your business from any other) and we are talking here about businesses that produce or sell similar products or services. It could be a special feature of your business, or maybe an appealing offer.

Customers need a reason to select one business over another and your USP will provide them with the reason why they should choose your business ahead of your rivals'. This, of course, means that you must select something relevant to your target market.

 Your USP should be a short and snappy phrase or description. It should be clear and to the point, leaving nothing to misinterpretation.

It's vital that your USP is realistic and deliverable every time, to every customer.

Now, you may find this difficult to digest, but your USP doesn't have to be unique. It's all down to perception. For example, your competitors may be offering the same sort of products or services as you, but unless they emphasise them in their marketing, how will potential customers ever know? If you are the only business drawing attention to a particular feature of a product or service, it will appear to be your USP even if every business is offering the same feature.

When listing the ideas for your USPs for your business, be creative. Here are a few questions to help you pick them out:

- Where do you see yourself in a niche market?

- What features are your competitors offering?

- Why did your existing customer choose you?

- What does your targeted market group value above all else?

The secret of the most successful entrepreneurs is that they dare to be different.

Point of sale advertising

This is aimed at the impulse buyer. It can be a brochure or poster beside a cash register, or alongside a special sale item to draw the customer's attention to its existence. A prerequisite of an advertisement of this kind is for it to carry a money-off coupon or similar tempting inducement so that the customer can purchase the product immediately.

Sales posters in store windows are another example of point of sale advertising. In addition to persuading the public to purchase certain items, they are also enticing people into their store and to not walk by. By its very nature the content of this form of advertising needs to be eye-catching and it usually contains more visual content than the written word.

Direct mail

More commonly known as junk mail, if you are on the receiving end of it. Nevertheless, it's a form of advertising that works extremely well. There's no better way to get your product before a selected section of buyers than direct mail. This is where customer profiling really comes to the fore. It allows you to:

- target a selected group of buyers;
- aim your advertising at a predetermined area;
- stagger your sales campaign;
- control costs.

It therefore offers a greater chance of success for your campaign. Direct mail also permits you to keep existing customers abreast of new products or services. I consider this form of advertising ideal for new businesses, inasmuch as it's cost effective. It can be used by all types of firms, in either retailing or business-to-business sales. If you can't afford an extensive advertising campaign to build up a customer base, you can still buy or rent a mailing list to suit your pocket. Depending on the size of your proposed mailing, it's possible to negotiate generous discounts for postage from the Royal Mail.

Direct mail campaigns come in all sizes, from dentists reminding patients it's time for an inspection to recruitment agencies offering their services to human resources managers or aiming them directly at the consumer. Your mailshot can contain a single sales letter, or an elaborate brochure or catalogue. One of the advantages of this method of selling is that it can give you more control over the target area, and your budget.

There are firms that supply a complete mailing package which includes from designing and printing your material to actually putting it in the post for you. They will also follow it up at a later date and submit a marketing report to you, or simply supply you with a mailing list which can be downloaded from the internet.

Firms supplying mailing lists can be located either in the *Yellow Pages* or on the internet and their lists can either be bought outright or rented by:

- Business or profession type
- Job title
- Age groups or by birthdays
- Area
- Number of employees
- Sales volume

The above are but a few of the many examples of categories available. It's possible to rent or purchase a mailing list comprising finance directors, less than 40 years of age, employed in hi-tech companies by their birth dates. In fact, you name a combination to suit your business and it will be with you before you know it.

There are literally millions of households and business names and addresses available at any one time. With on demand and digital printing reducing costs, direct mail campaigns are available to the smallest business. Using a cautious step-by-step approach, direct mail provides an opportunity to promote and expand your business without the normal problems. It allows you to test your marketing, permitting removal of those parts of your sales strategy that don't work. Most of all, it provides you with flexibility.

The make up of your direct mail campaign can be either a letter and brochure or just a letter. There is no set dictate – each works equally well; it's simply a matter of choice. With a letter and brochure, the letter should do the selling and the accompanying leaflet should explain how your product or service works. Using the second method, your sales letter must do the work of both.

Writing a sales letter

Never write your letter thinking that it will end up in the waste bin. Put as much thought into your postal selling as any other form of promotion.

The most important part of a sales letter is its message and the letter needs a headline. This must emphasise your product or service's unique selling point. Knowing whom you are selling to is half the battle, so your market profile needs to be spot on.

If you are aiming at the grey market, keep a picture of someone over 60 in your mind and try to think as he would. Write to a specific reader and your letter will mean something. At least it will be read before it's trashed. Let's say you're selling shoes. Someone over 60 is more interested in comfort than fashion, but he still needs a pair of shoes that look smart. On the other hand, teenagers tend to place more reliance on fashion than comfort. To some youngsters the label can be a more powerful selling tool than the product itself.

A suitable headline for the type of firm shown in the case study and business plan in the Appendix might read as follows:

> **Fed up with customers always paying late? You can stop this problem right now!**

All small business owners/managers to whom the letter would be personally addressed have customers who are slow in paying their accounts. Unfortunately, too few have time to do anything about it as they are too busy running their businesses, so they may wish to outsource the credit control.

On the other hand, credit managers or finance directors of larger companies are also plagued by late payment as it's a problem that bears influence on their cash flow forecasts and profits. They too may be influenced by this headline if it's used by a debt-collecting agency.

 For best results, always fold your letter so that the headline is the first item to catch the eye as it's removed from the envelope and not a blank page.

As soon as a harassed small business owner reads the above headline, he knows there is someone offering to resolve his problem for him and the headline indicates urgency, so he will be tempted to read on. Ideally, enclosed with this letter should be a brochure listing all the firm's services and charges.

One of the most common mistakes people make when they are new to writing sales letters is that they tend to overwrite. They use three words when two will do. Unlike some things in life, size doesn't really matter. A one-page sales letter can produce more results than a rambling monologue. What really matters is that you get the right message across to your reader. If you have got the customer profile right, this will inform you of the recipient's main interests, so when you are writing your sales letter it should be like writing to an old friend.

Brochures

Leaflets or brochures are like adverts, except you have more room to display your wares. It also allows you to include a few technical details, but don't put too many or the reader will be turned off.

Brochures (or leaflets) have many uses. For example, they are ideal as a stand-alone point of sales literature for inclusion with a sales letter or as follow-up material for those customers seeking more information about your company and its products. A brochure is also cheaper to produce and post than a full-scale catalogue.

A simple, yet effective brochure can consist of an A4 sheet of paper or light card folded twice to form six pages. Providing you have access to a personal computer, it's possible to produce an effective tract quite cheaply.

When writing a sales brochure, here's a few points to remember regarding the front page. Like any other advertising material, it requires an eye-catching headline. Use brief words that will urge the reader to turn the page. If your business has a logo, this too must be prominently displayed on the cover and if room allows it, repeat it on the back. Details, such as your contact address, telephone numbers, fax and email address, together with the briefest résumé of your firm's history, should be located on the back page.

Always post sales literature and invoices first class.

Because there is more space in a brochure than any other form of advertising, this doesn't mean that you have to fill it with meaningless jargon. Only use sufficient words to tell your story – it's far better to use a larger font size and/or a picture to fill out your brochure as this will help retain your customer's interest.

With the advent of reasonably priced PCs, the production of quality brochures or leaflets is no longer the expensive exercise it once was. However, churning out the same old type of material as your competitors will not win you new customers. True, you must let prospective customers know about your business and its products, but do it in such a way that makes your sales literature stand out. It must be so interesting that people will want to read it from cover to cover and tell their friends about it.

In among your sales blurb, place snippets of interest. Photographs are always a good idea and add useful tips or an odd recipe or two, but only if it's relevant to your product or service. Naturally, these additional comments should enhance your goods or services and will differ depending on the type of business you are running. The size and content of this extra material will also vary depending on whether you are producing a brochure or a sales letter and if you can get a local celebrity involved, so much the better.

 When writing advertising copy, remember that people will buy the benefits your product or service gives them (e.g. a motorist with a puncture doesn't want to buy a new tyre; all he wants is to complete his journey).

The type of business you are in will usually dictate the form of your promotions. If your products or services are unique, or if there is some aspect of your business that is newsworthy, you could perhaps ask your trade press or local newspaper to publish an article about your business – this is 'public relations'. Editors are always on the lookout for interesting new stories to fill their pages and they will print information about your business if what you are doing benefits the community or is newsworthy. Local radio stations are often a part of the media overlooked by small businesses when it comes to promoting their firm, but radio stations are very interested in hearing about local business.

You might also be able to associate your firm with local charities or other good causes. Public relations are about creating awareness of your business, as opposed to inducing direct sales.

Designing a website

This form of media is proving a boon to many small and new businesses, offering endless opportunities. With a modestly-priced computer, the smallest firm can become an international trader overnight. What is more, the cost of getting online is falling with the advent of broadband. There is nothing that cannot be sold using any other form of advertising that you can't sell online. E-commerce holds no boundaries and shouldn't be ignored.

Designing a website is no different from any other form of advertisement. All the rules mentioned earlier apply, but it does need to be accessed easily. So, in addition to an eye-catching headline, you need a relevant easy-to-remember web address. Also, your web page will require keywords so that anyone surfing the web for the sort of products or services you're offering will be directed to your site if these keywords are typed into a search engine.

 Keeping text short and pictures simple will make your site easier to download.

Always outline how you visualise the web pages will look when they have been completed. This rule applies if you are creating the site yourself, or employing a designer. Either way it saves time and avoids misunderstandings. When planning your firm's site it's a good idea to spend a few hours looking at rival sites. Jot down the things you either liked or disliked about them; then work out how it can be done better.

 Design tip! Keep it simple. Make it as easy as possible for computer novices to access your site and navigate through it.

Web pages are written in a computer language called 'Hypertext Mark-up Language' (HTML). Using this idiom to build a website allows you to instruct the text and graphics to appear in a variety of formats. For instance, you could have your firm's logo bursting onto the screen like fireworks, the text could be cascading, or the headline could show itself first in one size and then expand until it fills the screen. However, when you are mapping out your site do avoid using too much colour or gimmicks as it can take the browser's eye away from your main message.

Worried about learning HTML? Don't be. These days you can design a professional looking website without resorting to using this language, just by using the abundance of software available. This software can be downloaded free of charge or it may already be loaded onto your computer, such as Microsoft's *Front Page*.

Apart from the normal displays and text, your website will require links. Links are buttons, pictures or icons that prompt anyone browsing your site to click to other pages of your site.

When designing your web pages don't forget to incorporate an order form which can be emailed to you. To do this you will need to be able to offer your customers a secure site and for you to be paid via credit or debit cards. Your bankers will provide information about merchant accounts, which allow these types of transactions to be conducted safely.

However, there is a downside to having more space at your disposal compared with a newspaper advertisement. Cramming your web pages with too much information can make it longer to load and your customers could easily get impatient and go to a competitor's site. On the other hand, web pages can easily be remoulded if they don't produce the size of results you hoped.

Designing your firm's image

If you are intending to design and create your own advertising literature, including your letter headings, business cards and logo, take a little time to think about the image you wish to create; for example, traditional style, value for money, exceptional service, etc. When designing your business image and sales literature do be constant. Never deviate or change your style halfway through as this will confuse your customers. You must think about all the different forms of literature you need, in addition to invoices and purchasing orders, debt-chasing letters, etc.

Concentrate your thoughts on how your product or service will benefit your purchaser. If you have more than one idea, just jot these thoughts down until you decide on the design you are comfortable with. Above all, don't:

- use information that quickly becomes dated;
- produce designs that will entail disproportionate costs;
- print the literature before checking the proofs.

Look at what your competitors are doing to get inspiration and then consider how you can make your narrative stand out. Legal requirements, such as company details on letter headings, should be given careful deliberation.

Finally, before going to print, assess the general impact and end product of the design. Get friends or relations to comment on whether they are eye-catching and convey the right type of image. Don't forget to ask everyone studying your material to point out any mistakes.

Getting customers to buy

As long as you have new and existing customers, the selling process should never stop. Always be prepared and be confident in your product or service. If you are selling directly to customers, make sure that you are addressing the decision-maker. Your time is valuable so don't waste it and when conducting a sale always strive to create a situation where both you and your customer come away from the encounter feeling satisfied with the result. Here are some pointers to ensure that this happens:

1. **Determine the customer's needs.** Ask questions that will encourage a conversation; not 'yes' or 'no' responses. Listen carefully to what your customer is saying. Discover which product or service you have that most meets his needs. A good listener will always outsell the glib sales patter of the most talkative salesperson.

2. **Emphasise the benefits.** Demonstrate to the customer how what you are selling meets his needs. Show how your product or service will bring real benefits to him.

3. **Close the sale.** Be polite but direct and ask for the business. Never hesitate when it comes to closing a sale and taking an order – you've probably spent much time and effort getting to this stage!

Always ask your customer why he bought your product or service, as you may be able to use this information in future sales. By the same token, if your customer didn't complete a purchase, try to discover why. It will help you to improve your sales technique or product in the future.

 More than any other reason why sales are lost is because the salesperson didn't actually ask for the order.

4. **If a customer wants to think it over, agree with him.** State that you are not surprised at his request and ask him what part of your product or service he wishes to think about. Use this opportunity to clear any doubts from his mind about what your product can do for him. Now try to close the sale again.

 If, at any time during your meeting with a customer, there is a silent pause, never be the first to break the silence if you want to make the sale, even if it feels like an eternity.

5. **Negotiate successfully.** You will need to be a good negotiator, whatever line of business you are in. Since all successful negotiations require some give and take from both sides, the following advice may be of help to you:

- Work out in advance the price beyond which you will not go and then stick to it.

- If questioned on price, explain confidently and clearly why your price is reasonable. Remember to explain the benefits.

- Never make compromises unless you are getting something in return; for example, 'I'll reduce the price by 2.5 per cent if you pay cash on delivery, or double your order.'

- If you are the buyer, give way on inexpensive concessions; for example, be flexible on delivery dates if the price is reduced.

It's this sort of bargaining that builds lasting business relationships. When negotiating, bear in mind that what is regarded as unimportant to you could, in fact, be valuable to the other party.

A golden rule in any business or sales environment is never turn up at a potential or existing customer's home or office without a prior appointment. You can never know what urgent problem your customer may be dealing with at the time. Whatever it is, it will certainly be more important to him than your products or services. So, be professional, arrange an appointment to see him; again at the time of your call he may be busy, so ask if it's a convenient time to talk. Mornings are usually a good time to telephone business customers. Call as early as possible before they get tied up in their day-to-day business problems. Your customers will respect your business approach.

 The key to selling your products or services is to discover what the buyer wants and help him to get it.

Telephoning for an appointment is preferable to writing a letter. The aim of your telephone call is to get a time and place to meet your customer – nothing else. Certainly don't try to sell your product or service until you meet. To make things easier for yourself and get round secretaries, ask for the person you wish to see by name, if possible using his first name. Avoid job titles if at all possible. The main steps to selling are as follows:

1. Plan your approach. Find out as much about your customers as you can and before making contact be sure you know what you wish to achieve.

2. When you are face to face with your customer, treat him considerately, engage his interest and be persistent.

3. Ask questions and get the customer in the habit of saying 'yes'. Identify how your product or service fits the customer's requirements. Listen carefully – this can be more important than talking.

4. Handle objections confidently. Show the customer that you take his objection seriously. Isolate, test and address his objections. The most

common objection is price. Emphasise on the quality of your prod or service. Stress the after-sales service or other benefits you may offering.

5. Close the sale. Look for buying signals such as, 'When would you able to deliver?' or 'What other colour can you supply?' Tal responsibility for closing the sale. The simplest way may be to just as if you can take his order now. Other examples might be the following

   - If I can guarantee to bring the delivery date forward, will you place an order now?

   - If the buyer asks the price, respond by asking if that is the product he will buy.

   - When only one objection remains, make the sale conditional upon removing that obstacle.

Discuss your product or service enthusiastically. Enthusiasm is catching and does more to build lasting rapport with your customer than anything else. Other points to remember are to maintain eye contact and encourage your customer to ask questions. Before closing, recap on what has been discussed and once the sale is agreed, confirm everything in writing.

 Never berate the competition; it suggests that your contact's judgement is flawed.

Any sales literature you wish to leave with the customer should be handed over as you leave. You don't want to distract him from what you are saying.

Terms of trade

When a customer purchases goods or services from your business, you have entered into a legal contract. Therefore it's imperative that your terms of trade are clearly displayed to avoid any misunderstandings arising. Customers have statutory rights and can reasonably expect the goods:

- to be of satisfactory quality to perform their intended purpose;

- to match any description given of them.

If you make any factual claims about the product prior to completing the contract, which can be either written or oral, that prove to be untrue and the purchaser can prove he based his decision to buy upon your statements, then he may be able to make a claim against you.

Furthermore, if your terms are considered to be unfair, the consumer doesn't have to be bound by them. However, this doesn't cover the terms that set the price.

All terms and conditions of sale should be expressed in an easy-to-understand language and clearly documented. This 'small print' should be included on the back of all invoices, order forms and any other relevant documentation. This especially applies to the term of payment so the purchaser is under no illusion about how much he is expected to pay, when and where payment is to be made.

 If you are selling goods by weight, the unit price must be displayed.

When describing or selling a service you must not make any false or misleading statements about the service you are offering, nor should you exaggerate on the size of your business or its capabilities.

Selling your goods or services correctly is covered by straightforward guidelines. Make sure that you act responsibly and give both you and your customer a fair deal.

There are many more terms of trade that you should follow in addition to the above examples. For more information about trade descriptions and terms of trade, I urge you to contact your local Trading Standards Office or visit its website at www.tradingstandards.gov.uk.

Looking after existing customers

You've started your business and overcome more than a few teething problems, so let's now assume that it's up and running. But after the initial flood of customers, suddenly and without any explanation sales reach a plateau. This can be frustrating, but you must not lose sight of your existing customers. Always make sure that they remain with you as this is a far more cost effective way of doing business.

Now don't get me wrong, getting a constant stream of new customers to your door is vital to every business, but it's very costly.

 The best way to increase sales is to convince your present customers to buy other products or services from you.

Turning new customers into loyal ones is the key to maximising the returns on your marketing investment and customer service is the way to do it. Get this right and although there will always be a need for advertising your business, this will diminish in time as more and more of your existing customers do the marketing for you via referrals.

Always go out of your way to let your existing customers know that you appreciate their custom. Some businesses use loyalty cards offering discounts on future purchases, others have 'Air Miles', while another may offer a money-off coupon when buying a certain number of litres of petrol, for example. There are many avenues you can explore to come up with ideas that will let your customers know that they are wanted.

One other method that will not cost you a penny is to greet your customer by name every time he calls into your place of business. Not all businesses can do this, simply because of the large number of customers walking through their doors. Most small businesses should be able to use this ploy, at the expense of their bigger rivals.

Every business needs a customer service agenda

This will help you achieve customer satisfaction and every member of your staff should be involved, not just those in the front line, such as sales and marketing. Your accounts people, warehouse and packing staff are all part of the team and while some of them may not have direct contact with the customer their actions can reflect on how the customer sees your business. For example, a badly-packed item may arrive broken or cracked simply because the person responsible for packing it didn't take enough care. A customer telephoning to complain about this may be answered with a surly 'couldn't care less' attitude. These types of incidents can add up to an unsatisfied customer.

The goal of good customer service is to avoid losing a customer to a competitor.

What should your customer service agenda set out to achieve and what is the best way forward? When introducing a customer service agenda you must take the ensuing steps:

1. **Identify your most valuable customers.** You can do this simply by using the 80/20 'rule of thumb' guide. This equates to 20 per cent of your customers purchasing 80 per cent of your products or services.

2. **Discover the level of service they require.** Customer satisfaction surveys are the best way to achieve this. If your business attracts different groups of customers, carry out separate surveys for each group. These surveys should draw your attention to the:

    *   quality of service you are offering;

    *   satisfaction customers have with the facilities (methods of payment, parking, etc.);

    *   staff's attitude and behaviour;

    *   handling of complaints.

    The above indicators are just a few of the main issues you should be concentrating on. To complete your lists consider other topics, such as communications and the level of service customers have a right to expect (e.g. professional, courteous and prompt service, which includes competent and well-trained staff) plus fair prices for quality products and/or services. Always ensure that customers have your full and exclusive attention when they decide to do business with you and make sure that your appreciation for their continued custom is clearly evident.

 Avoid vagueness when publishing your customer service agenda. Instead of insisting that incoming telephone calls should be answered promptly, state that they should be answered within two or three rings.

3. **Develop a customer service standards programme.** Build into your standards a level of service that reflects your surveys' findings; a

level that will ensure customer loyalty and long-term satisfaction. To assist you it's important that everyone (your management team, all staff members and above all your customers) are involved in developing your standards. Train your staff in the importance of above-average customer service and try to deliver a personalised service when and where possible.

- Review customer service standards regularly.

- Service standards should be produced in a clear and concise manner.

- Ensure that service standards are achievable and measurable.

- Reward good service and contributions to the programme.

These rewards need not be very costly. A gift voucher from a local department store or a half-day holiday are just two examples of low-cost methods of reward.

Dealing with customer complaints

One of the best gauges of the success of your business is the number of customer complaints you receive and how you deal with them. Ignore your customer complaints at your peril because they can tell you more about your business than anything else. They will instantly point to problems with the product or service you are offering and when this is brought to your attention, act upon the information straight away as this will reduce the level of complaints you will receive in the future. As soon as a customer takes the trouble to complain, you should:

- acknowledge receipt of the letter or telephone call;

- tell the customer the timescale within which you expect to be able to deal with the problem; and

- thank the customer for bringing the problem to your attention.

Make sure that the member of staff dealing with the customer's complaint is confident and aware that the firm's management will support his decisions.

note It's imperative that you talk to your customers, but it's more important to listen to what they have to say.

It's vital that you record all complaints as they surface, as well as tracking them through the system until they are resolved to the customer's satisfaction and in the shortest timeframe possible.

Customer service and complaint handling are areas where small businesses can outshine their larger rivals. Small business owners/managers are closer to their customers and can respond more rapidly when something goes wrong.

Existing customers should be important to you and you must not neglect them for the sake of getting new ones through the door. Let them be aware of your customer service agenda and remove any obstacles you can which prevent them from doing business with you.

What about the customer from hell?

Most customers who complain have genuine grievances. However, they generally like doing business with you and your products or services meet their needs. If you recognise this in a customer and act accordingly, you have a loyal client to cherish and a long-lasting and profitable relationship will develop.

But what happens when you meet the customer from hell; the one who complains endlessly and always pays late? The first thing you must decide is whether:

- he has a real complaint; or
- is he just being awkward?

If your customer does have a real complaint, dealing with his problem will give you an opportunity to strengthen your relationship with that customer.

However, if the customer is simply being awkward or using it as an excuse to delay payment, then you must decide whether he is the type of customer you want. This type of customer may well be using up your valuable resources which could be profitably used elsewhere in your organisation, and if this is the case, then you may be happy to lose his business.

The best way to respond to such a customer is to be polite and simply tell him that it's obvious that he will never be satisfied with your business or its products and it is time for him to look for another supplier.

Nonetheless, it's important to distinguish between the two types of customer – the one with the genuine complaint and the other who is not worth trying to please. If you receive a series of complaints from the first example, perhaps it's time to adapt your product or service to meet his requirements.

 It's impossible to be all things to all people, so don't try to be.

CHAPTER 4

Do you have sufficient resources?

What you'll find in this chapter

✔ Operations
✔ Premises
✔ Fire protection
✔ Managing waste
✔ Equipment
✔ Health and safety
✔ Reporting accidents
✔ Stock and suppliers
✔ Key personnel and skill shortages
✔ Training
✔ Getting the most from your resources

From this point onwards, you should be considering what resources you currently have and those you will need in the future. At first, you may be able to work alone, maybe from home, but you will need premises and personnel assistance once your business takes off. Working from home may sound like fun, but you must learn to separate your business from your home life at the end of the day. Certainly this arrangement will reduce your start-up costs, but there will be drawbacks as well. For example, those with whom you share your living premises may not appreciate giving up 'their' space and may find it difficult being restricted by the close proximity of your work. Customers who visit unexpectedly could prove a hindrance to a happy family life. Furthermore, you may find it hard to stop working and relax when the day is done.

Working from home can also have financial disadvantages. You may have to pay business-rate Council Tax on your home. To find out if running a business from your home will increase your tax, contact either your local branch of the Valuation Office Agency or go online at www.voa.gov.uk. If you sell your house, Capital Gains Tax may be levied. There may also be restricted covenants in your mortgage document or tenancy agreement excluding certain activities. An accountant and solicitor will be able to advise you on these matters.

Before you set up your business at home, check with your local authority and your household insurance policy again for any restrictions against the arrangement. Your business equipment, for example, may not be covered by your existing insurance policy. You are advised to carry out a health and safety risk assessment before you start trading. This equally applies wherever you decide to set up your business.

Your financial forecasts will have to take into consideration your future requirements in respect of employing or increasing staff, in addition to ensuring any separate business premises you may require when expanding your business is suitable and has been properly costed.

 Here is a rule of thumb guide for working from home: provided your business doesn't create noise or smells and doesn't cause congestion, of either people or vehicles, there should be no major problem. Whatever you do, it's advisable to keep on good terms with your neighbours.

Operations

How you intend to operate will need to be included in your overall business plan. This plan will present information to any interested party about the resources you have or will require to achieve your marketing aim and predicted sales targets. You may, for instance, need to cover seasonal fluctuations by using temporary staff or subcontractors, and this must be made evident.

There are obvious pros and cons to running your business from separate premises. On the positive side, a clear professional image would be gained.

Your work will also be more self-contained and less likely to encroach on your private life. One considerable disadvantage is the greater risk of theft or vandalism; with no one on the premises overnight, you will need to budget for security measures.

Many people starting out in business use only their own finance. Others need to borrow until their turnover builds up sufficiently. Borrow too much, and you will pay too much interest. Borrow too little, and you will be unable to meet your expenses. There is a fine line between these last two and you will need to budget carefully.

If you need to borrow to get started, do make sure that your calculations are correct. You must also be confident that your business will generate enough profits to repay any loans within the agreed terms. Don't forget to communicate this confidence to the lender as well! It's possible to produce an accurate assessment of what you will need as well as your ability to repay any loan. A well-prepared cash flow forecast, explained in chapter 6, will show a comparison of your income and expenditure on a monthly basis over the next few years. You will also find a few more ideas and requirements that will get the bank manager on your side in chapter 7.

Premises

Previously, we have taken an overview of the pros and cons of the location of your business. However, for the purpose of this next section, we have assumed that you will operate away from your home environment. Whichever arrangement you decide upon, make sure that your business will have sufficient room to grow.

Business premises can be acquired under different guises, some of which are listed here for your information. However you wish to operate, there will be one method to suit you.

- **Freehold or long leasehold purchase.** Since mortgage costs can fluctuate from one extreme to another, this option may contain too many hidden dangers for a start-up business. Purchasing, meanwhile, can also be a drawback if you expand rapidly and you are unable to move into larger premises. It's probably prudent to leave this option until your business is well established.

- **Rental or leasing.** Leasing retail, commercial or industrial property on a fixed term is the usual method for obtaining business premises. All property leases will contain conditions to insure the premises. There may also be restrictions on its use. Make sure that you understand the terms before signing.

- **Property licence.** This is available to all businesses, but it's of particular interest to new businesses, and is often referred to as 'easy in, easy out'. Using business premises on licence enables either party to terminate the agreement at a relatively short notice, such as one to three months. This is beneficial to you if you don't know how long you will require the premises, but the arrangement could prove inconvenient if your landlord issues notice and you want to remain in the premises because it suits you and it's convenient for your customers. However, occupying a property licence does allow you to move into larger premises quickly as your business grows.

> The correct site for your business is vital for your business survival. Spend time thinking about the best position for you before committing yourself.

Take expert advice from a surveyor and solicitor before entering into a contract to rent or buy premises. The condition of commercial premises is important as well as its suitability for the type of business you are proposing. Remember that you will be responsible for the upkeep of the premises as most landlords will only offer a full repairing and insuring lease agreement. Surveyors will also assist you in ensuring that:

- planning approval for your intended use of the building is obtained, if required;

- any changes you propose making comply with building regulations;

- you provide easy access for disabled people.

Access for your customers, and sometimes your suppliers, is a very important consideration when deciding upon your location. A retailer will benefit in a location where people frequently pass his door. Commercial premises will need easy access or have adequate car parking facilities. Think of the advantage of being situated next to a railway station!

Industrial premises, on the other hand, may be better situated close to a motorway or on an industrial estate.

Fire protection

Fire protection is another important issue that needs to be addressed. Since 2006 fire certificates have been abolished, but all businesses are required to carry out a fire risk assessment and demonstrate that they have proper controls in place. Guidance on this subject can be obtained from the fire safety officer based at your local fire station. Business premises must meet certain standards for the safety of their staff and customers and you will need the following:

- Adequate escape routes
- Fire resistant door and walls
- Sufficient fire fighting equipment
- Fire alarms
- Emergency lighting

You will also be required to provide safe storage for flammable materials and provide adequate training for your staff.

Managing waste

Any waste your business generates is your responsibility. Good waste management saves money and benefits the environment. When dealing with waste you must store it in suitable sacks, skips or containers and ensure that they are safe.

All waste collected from your business premises must be disposed of correctly by an authorised waste collector or local council. At the time your waste is removed from your premises, you are required to complete a waste disposal transfer note, which will describe the waste and state its origin. You must keep this document for two years. For hazardous waste, the consignment note must be retained for three years.

Special rules and registration requirements apply for toxic and hazardous waste, so if your business will be using or producing anything of this nature, you need to seek advice from the Environment Agency at www. environment-agency.gov.uk.

Manufacturers and retailers producing or selling electrical and electronic goods must comply with the Waste Electronic and Equipment Directive (WEEE), which states that measures must be introduced to allow customers to return items for disposal.

If your business entails transporting materials, including those mentioned above, do refer to the licensing requirements discussed in chapter 1.

Equipment

All businesses need some form of equipment to enable them to make a profit. But it's not necessary for the business to own that equipment, thus tying up money that could profitably be used elsewhere. Most business equipment can be leased or rented, which then allows you to use it and make a profit from it without actually owning it. Further information on this can be found in chapter 7.

So whether you just require a desk and a computer, perhaps a van or car, or shelving and counters for a retail business, make sure that the equipment you acquire is right for its proposed function and safe to use. This also applies to machinery bought by manufacturers, restaurateurs and every other type of business.

 There are specific regulations to ensure that equipment is maintained and checked regularly. Contact www.hse.gov.uk to ensure that you are complying with these regulations.

Employees must be properly trained on every piece of equipment and you will be responsible for minimising the risks to avoid accidents occurring.

Computers are another area of concern and they must be used safely. As well as checking that visual display units (VDUs) and keyboards allow users to work comfortably, you are also required to ensure that employees get regular breaks. On-screen characters must be clear with adequate spacing and the screen image must not flicker. Other requirements are as follows:

- The keyboard must be separate from the screen.

- The screen must be tiltable.

- The computer must be positioned in a way that it avoids fatigue to arms and hands.

The operator's chair must be stable and the seat back adjustable for both height and tilt. Workstation layouts need to be planned to prevent glare or reflections on the screen and must give the operator ample space to vary his movements or change position.

 Breaks from computer use should be allowable at least every two hours.

Regular eye tests paid for by you should be offered at frequent intervals or when they are requested. It's essential to avoid mistakes by providing sufficient training in the use of software.

Having sufficient equipment, including office and/or works machinery, to carry on your business is another aspect to bear in mind. Equipment already owned by you can be brought into the business and charged at a reasonable rate. Anything owned outright will become an asset of the business and will increase its worth. Equipment naturally loses its value as it gets older or becomes obsolete, so it will need to be replaced. This is called 'depreciation'.

Its reliability, condition and service life needs to be stressed within the body of your business plan. This is essential if you wish to ensure the profitability of your business.

Plans for transportation and distribution must also be considered before setting up your business. For instance, do you have a sufficient number of vehicles and are these vehicles suitable for achieving your goals? When producing your profit and loss forecasts the costs of running all your motor vehicles must be stated, in addition to the details of their ownership.

With regard to any vehicle used for your trade, it's advisable to keep business and private use separate. The taxman will insist upon this.

If you need to deliver products to your customers, investigate the cost of outside contractors. It may prove more cost effective to use their services than to purchase your own vehicles.

Health and safety

Health and safety laws affect all businesses, some more so than others. These rules don't only apply to employers. Employees, including those gaining work experience and volunteers, are equally responsible for ensuring that accidents are reduced to a minimum in the workplace. If you don't think that health and safety issues involve you because you are self-employed or you work from home, then think again. These laws exist to protect all employees and employers alike.

 By adhering to health and safety regulations, businesses can avoid losing valuable staff at crucial times due to unnecessary accidents.

If you employ staff, then you need a health and safety policy concerning those aspects of the law affecting your type of business. Your employees must be kept up to date and involved with the procedure. The health and safety regulations applicable to the type of business you run must be displayed for all to see.

If you are unable to oversee health and safety in your business, then you must appoint someone to do this task. It's also compulsory that suitable first aid facilities are available and all staff need to be aware of where the first aid boxes are located. A responsible person must be nominated and trained on how to perform first aid, restock the first aid boxes and, if necessary, call for an ambulance.

The Health and Safety Executive can help you with these regulations. You are urged to view its website at www.hse.gov.uk to see what is appropriate for your actual business. It's possible to download any regulations appropriate to your business free of charge.

Reporting accidents

Most accidents that happen in the workplace usually involve some form of equipment. All serious injuries or accidents that do occur, and this includes illnesses, are to be recorded in an accident book with the date and details of each incident together with the name of the injured person. This also applies to customers and other visitors to your premises. Near misses also must be logged.

Specific incidents must be reported to the Health and Safety Executive or your local council, which include:

- deaths or major injuries;
- certain work-related illnesses;
- any incident that causes someone to be off work for more than three days.

The special records you will be required to keep are covered by the Reporting of Injuries, Diseases and Dangerous Occurrences Regulations (RIDDOR). To keep up to date on any changes to these rules and to report incidents, visit the Incident Contact Centre online at www.riddor.gov.uk.

Stock and suppliers

Stock and materials are two other resources that must be considered when completing your business plan. If these are central to your business operation, then you must be sure of getting supplies when you need them and at a price you can afford. You will also need to ensure that raw materials will be of a consistent quality and high standard.

Because the cost of materials is important to the success of your business, do obtain quotations from as many different suppliers as possible. Next, use these quotations to convince one supplier to offer you the best deal, such as reduced prices or extended credit. Your business statement should contain the following points:

- The importance of materials to your business.

- The reliability of your suppliers – do they deliver on time?

- Is the quality of supplier constant?

It's vital to the survival of your business that you continually review your suppliers and the service they give you. By monitoring the prices they charge and ensuring that the goods you order are delivered on time will in turn keep your business competitive. If costs start to rise unreasonably or the service begins to flag and your orders arrive late, look for a new supplier.

When you do find a reliable supplier, don't simply accept the first price he quotes, haggle. Ask for 2.5 per cent or five per cent off for prompt payment; perhaps you will get more for guaranteeing regular orders. Negotiating lower prices is an art so to assist you, here are a few handy tips:

- Don't start bargaining until you are sure that you want the goods or services.

- Don't give away the price you are prepared to pay.

- Never give way on a point without getting something in return.

- Keep quiet – the one who is speaking is giving away his position.

- Confirm everything agreed in writing.

Remember, every pound you save is better in your pocket than in your supplier's.

TIP To be sure of a reliable supply of raw materials, use more than one supplier.

If the raw materials used in your business are imported, keep a constant eye on the political situation of the country of origin. Any sudden change in government or its policies could be devastating to your business. Be prepared to shift your order elsewhere by having alternative suppliers in other less volatile regions to hand.

Key personnel and skill shortages

Before you progress very far with your business plan, clarify what sort of key personnel you must have to get your business off the ground. Are you looking to be the owner of a sole trading company, or do you require partners for a partnership or directors of a limited company? In addition to these essential roles, there may be others who will be central to your business success, such as employees or associates.

A brief CV or a career profile of every person who will be playing a leading role in your business should be included in your business plan. The basic information you need to present on these people is as follows:

- Names and qualifications.
- Relevant experience and trade knowledge.
- How their skills will contribute to the success of the business.

This data should be incorporated into an 'executive summary' and form part of your operation strategy. A typical career profile can be seen in the case study and specimen business plan in the Appendix.

Keep your business plan updated in respect of new and existing key personnel, especially with regard to training or new qualifications.

Changing markets, new technology and an expanding business all mean maintaining and improving the skill levels of your employees on a continual basis. There are three ways to address this problem: outsourcing, recruiting additional staff and identifying skill shortages.

1. **Outsourcing or subcontracting.** This option will ensure that you have experienced people completing specific tasks for a pre-set period. Payment is often made only when certain targets have been met. The working arrangement between the parties ceases on completion of the contract. Outsourcing may remove your liability for payment of National Insurance contributions, sick leave and holidays. However, the rates of pay are likely to exceed those of your directly employed staff. Another potential problem to be aware of is that outsourced contractors will lack familiarity with your firm's operations and standards.

2. **Recruiting.** In order to justify taking on extra people on a full- or part-time basis, you will need to group skill requirements into a job description. A job description (or specification) provides the facts about the job – its basic function and responsibilities – as well as a brief explanation as to where the employee slots into the chain of command. The job description should also include the required skills and experience the prospective employee should possess. A good personnel specification and job description will go a long way towards helping you get the right person for the job.

Remember that if you are employing temporary staff directly, you must accord them the same employment rights as full-time workers.

3. **Identifying skill shortages.** There may be some aspects of your new business that will be strange to you. For example, you may know little about book-keeping, but book-keeping is only an extension of keeping a household budget. Although it's a little more complex, the principles are the same. So whatever the 'grey area', your local training and enterprise agency will be able to help. Just pick up the phone!

The areas in which a new business may experience skill shortages fall into the following categories:

- **Financial.** Includes bought and sales ledgers, general book-keeping, VAT, PAYE, balance sheets and budgeting.

- **Sales and marketing.** Covers personal selling skills, market research, advertising, customer care and product designing.

- **Personnel and management.** Involves managing time and people, target setting, industrial relations, training, staff appraisals, dismissal and grievance procedures.

- **Operations and communications.** Embraces production planning, stock control, computer systems, presentation and report writing.

- **General skills.** Incorporates company law, business planning and secretarial.

- **Technical and professional.** Embodies all of those skills specific to the type of business you are in; for example, plumbing, interior design, childcare, engineering and bricklaying.

The above list only represents a small proportion of the skills required to run and sustain business growth.

 Ask yourself if you have the right people, with the right skills, in the right place, at the right time, to deliver your marketing plan.

Training

Provision for ongoing training should be part of your continual business strategy. An explicit schedule, either for yourself or for staff, will be a prerequisite for the skill shortage you have chosen to meet through training. By drawing up such a document, you will have a clear mental picture of the total costs and hours involved, as well as the end result of such instruction. This is precisely the sort of information that must be communicated to potential investors. A typical training programme will identify:

- the skills being taught;
- the names of the trainees;
- the teaching methods; for example, own or external staff;
- the tutor and location.

 There are a great many training incentives available to businesses today, via government-sponsored schemes.

Training can range from brief instructions followed by a period of supervision (e.g. showing a new employee how to operate a particular piece of machinery) to much longer-term methods (e.g. working towards a National Vocational Qualification (NVQ) or a professional qualification). To demonstrate the importance of training in business, the 'Investors in People' initiative was set up to encourage ongoing training. 'Investors in People' is a national award presented to businesses that demonstrate commitment and attain definite standards in training. Firms participating in this initiative are required to develop employees' skills in order to achieve the objectives outlined in their business plan. A sample training plan is to be found in the case study in the Appendix.

Personnel development and training builds confidence and motivates staff. Their improved performance will be reflected in your profits. Making people's skills work involves an ongoing training schedule to be put into place and reviewed at regular intervals. It's the only sure-fire way to ensure that your business is around in the future and not languishing in past glory.

Getting the most from your resources

Planning ahead and trying to predict what additional equipment or staff you may need as your business grows will help you to get maximum use of your existing resources. The right mix of personnel, premises and fiscal resources is crucial to the success of your business.

CHAPTER 5

Recruiting and managing staff

What you'll find in this chapter

- ✔ Recruiting employees
- ✔ Job descriptions
- ✔ Employment contracts
- ✔ Conducting staff appraisals
- ✔ Managing performance
- ✔ Disciplinary and grievance procedures
- ✔ Letting people go
- ✔ Staff handbooks

Employing people for the first time can be a daunting experience. There are more rules and regulations to trip you up when hiring and firing than in any other part of your business. But there will come a time when you will need to employ people, maybe not in the beginning, but as your business grows. When you were an employee, you had no reason to worry about recruitment procedures, but now you need to know about the pros and cons of taking on staff and managing their performance.

Taking on people to assist you to run your business will remove some of the mundane tasks from your shoulders and will allow you to manage your business more effectively. However, these employees will bring with them extra responsibilities and obligations. The rules relating to conditions of employment are numerous and complex. Minimum wage and maternity leave are just two examples; other rights concerning employees include:

- health and safety;
- unfair dismissal;
- redundancy;
- flexible working and job sharing;
- discrimination on the grounds of sex, race, sexual orientation, religion or belief, marital status, disability and age.

There is the added burden of ensuring that the people you employ can work in the UK. The Home Office can help you with this; just visit www.ind.homeoffice.gov.uk.

 It's essential that you insure your staff against accident or illness while they are on company time.

Taking on your first member of staff is a huge step, but this chapter will help you think through the recruitment and appointment process while at the same time focusing on what is best for your business.

Recruiting employees

The people you employ will become ambassadors of your business and in many instances will be the first face your customers will see. Selecting the right recruits is therefore crucial, but it's not as easy as it may sound.

Small businesses are able to move faster than their larger competitors. Selecting someone who is adaptable and able to grow with your business should be your first priority. While experience and knowledge of the type of business you operate may seem an ideal attribute when employing someone, if the applicant has only worked in a big business environment, he may feel ill at ease once the support mechanism of a larger company is taken away. He may have been a huge success in his previous position, but is unable to function in a small business setting. There are now no easy options for him, nowhere to hide and no quiet days when working in a small firm and this can be a very demanding experience.

A probationary period of three to six months is the best way to ensure that new employees fit in and also to test their adaptability, thus avoiding costly mistakes.

If you have partners or fellow directors, every one of them must be in agreement on the selected candidate. If just one of them is unhappy with a particular person, then that should be reason enough to pass him over.

 Remember that you can train someone without the right skills or give him experience, but there is little you can do if he is not adaptable.

Before inserting your first recruitment advertisement or appointing a recruitment agency, make sure that you are clear about the skills, experience and attitude you are looking for in your first employee. Furthermore, you must know exactly what tasks you require him to undertake within your business. Composing a job description will assist you in this matter.

Job descriptions

When recruiting general staff a job description doesn't have to be sent to prospective employees, but one should be created for your own use and if you are using a recruitment agency. The contents of the job description should be discussed at the interview stage and will assist you when you are discussing the position on offer with the recruits.

 If you are using a recruitment agency, get it to confirm that it understands what you are looking for. Make it prepare a shortlist of candidates and, above all else, haggle over fees.

However, if you are hiring senior level members of staff (e.g. from supervisors upwards) or want to fill vacancies requiring technical or special skills, sending out an application pack including a job description is essential to avoid unsuitable candidates applying and wasting your time.

An example of how a typical job description may be constructed can be found below.

Job Description
Job title:
Location:
Salary:
Responsible to:
Purpose of the job:
Key responsibilities/tasks:
Knowledge, skills and attainments:
Essential:
Preferable (or willing and able to develop):
Measures of good performance:
Working relationships:
Internal:
External:

Once you have hired a member of staff, as the business owner you must define clearly his respective role within the business. Your new employee will then feel that he has a real role to play and is a valuable member of the team. Furthermore, it's important that he knows that his ideas or suggestions are important to the success of the business and that he will be listened to and respected.

 Some employers prefer candidates to complete a job application form, while others are happy with just a CV. Some prefer to use both. There are no set rules on this so just do what suits you best.

From the moment that you offer the most suitable candidate a position in your business and he accepts the job, a contract has been entered into. Both of you are now obligated to the terms of that contract and although the contract will probably be verbal initially, it's nevertheless as binding as the written contract that you will give to him.

Employment contracts

One thing that you must never overlook when employing staff are contracts of employment. These can be either written, verbal or implied. The contract can be conditional, perhaps depending on the receipt of references and/or a medical report. Most businesses provide a formal written contract, but all that is legally required is that you must give the employee a statement within two months of him joining the business. Among other things, the contract or statement will contain basic details such as the following:

- The employee's name.

- The employee's job title – it's a good idea to attach a job specification to the contract.

- The date employment started.

- The employee's working hours and holiday entitlement.

- Details of pay including commission payments and any bonuses, if applicable, together with information on how these are earned.

- The period of notice required to end employment.

- Sick pay and pensions.

When you are discussing pay with your new or existing employees, keep in mind the national minimum hourly wage. As this tends to increase each year, it's advisable to check the current rate by visiting www.hmrc.gov.uk.

There are a number of other important factors to be embodied within the contract of employment or employee handbook. Disciplinary and grievance procedures are just two examples and because of their importance these are covered in a separate section later in this chapter.

Employment contracts also give you certain rights as an employer and every contract should be made up of:

- statutory rights – such as those mentioned above;

- contractual rights – these are the rights which are expressed in the contract and can vary from business to business. There are two types of contractual rights:

1. **Express terms.** These are terms specifically agreed between employer and employee, some of which have been detailed above.

2. **Implied terms.** These are terms not specifically agreed, but they are implied or too obvious to be written down. For example, you will undertake to pay your staff for their endeavours and take care of their health and safety needs. On the other hand, you will naturally expect your employees to carry out their duties to the best of their ability, to be honest and obey reasonable instructions.

Employment contracts are now a permanent feature of business life and advice should be sought when drawing up your first contracts to avoid you facing expensive legal claims when an employee is required to leave. Fortunately, legal advice should not cost you the earth because good sources of free and low-cost legal assistance are just a mouse click away on the internet.

 You will need to get your employee's consent if you want to amend his employment contract.

Lawpack's *Employment Contracts Kit* and *Employment Law Made Easy* book can help by providing you with employment contract templates and background information. For further details, visit www.lawpack.co.uk.

When employing part-time workers they should not be treated less favourably than full-time staff and the same applies to those with disabilities. This means that they are entitled to the same rates of pay and holiday entitlement (pro rata, naturally) as well as having equal access to promotion opportunities, pension schemes and training.

 You cannot penalise employees for joining or not joining a union – employees don't need your permission.

Maternity and paternity leave are one of the many aspects to be taken into consideration when employing staff and their rights need to be stated in either the contract of employment, the statement of employment or an employee handbook.

Prior to taking on your very first member of staff you are strongly advised to check out the information on handbooks freely available from the

Advisory, Conciliation and Arbitration Service (ACAS), which can be found on its website at www.acas.org.uk.

Conducting staff appraisals

As the number of people you employ grows in line with the progress your business is making, you will come to appreciate those employees who take a pride in their work. This pride will not stem from the great products or services your business offers, but from the motivation they get from their employers. Firms that encourage staff to put forward ideas and provide ongoing training to develop the full potential of their employees are the businesses that thrive. This is why conducting staff appraisals and having an open door policy where staff and customers are concerned will pay dividends. It will be your job as an employer to recruit and retain good staff and you can only achieve this by having a reputation for treating staff well.

 A happy workforce is good for business – this is one maxim you must never forget.

By creating an atmosphere within your business in which staff can use their initiative to change the way they work, your employees will develop confidence, which in turn will help you to retain a loyal workforce. Furthermore, businesses that offer pleasant, inspiring workplaces in addition to treating their staff well suffer less from sickness and absenteeism. These last two factors can place a terrible strain on the finances of all businesses, especially new and small ones.

A new employee should have a reasonable period of induction into his job and the company and during the first year of employment should be appraised on a regular basis. You should appraise him at least monthly during the first three months, then quarterly and half-yearly gaps, followed by annual appraisals. However, do always have an open door policy which allows employees to feel free to approach you or, if applicable, their supervisors or managers at any time should the need arise.

Before conducting an appraisal it's essential that both you and your employee understand the benefits of the appraisal and its purpose, which are to:

- agree performance objectives;
- develop a training and development plan;
- set standards;
- disperse any doubts or fears the employee may have about his role in your business.

When setting performance objectives be SMART, i.e. all objectives should be:

Specific – Measurable – Achievable – Realistic – Time-framed

The objectives should always be agreed between the employer and employee and must never be imposed. They should be focused on improvement, at the same time ensuring that the standards are constant with similar roles within the company. The appraisal should also incorporate the employee's personal aspirations and develop a sense of accountability into his work. The following chart will assist you to agree objectives with your own employees:

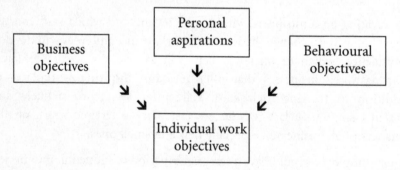

One outcome of any appraisal will be the development of a training programme for your employee to assist him with attaining his aspirations. Because training can be expensive for both the business and employee in both time and money, it's important that sound consideration is given to drawing up a proper training schedule and not a wish list.

 To help with the cost of training, check out those courses that are free from local Adult Training Centres and central and local government grants.

When you are establishing the priorities of a training plan, think about what:

- will help employees to do their job more effectively in future;
- is required by the employment regulations;
- could prepare employees for promotion;
- would motivate the employees to be more committed.

Once you have established these priorities, it's important to both the business and the employee that you offer the employee sufficient paid leave to attend the respective course or workshop. As well as guaranteeing free time to study, the type and method of training is equally important. Is the aim of the training to obtain academic or vocational qualifications (NVQs)? Will external or internal training be more resourceful? Perhaps job shadowing, coaching or mentoring is the answer. One solution that can work well for small businesses is online training; it's reasonably priced and workers can learn wherever and whenever it suits you.

 Make sure that your employees feel that they are part of a team and not isolated; fragmentation is bad for business.

When it comes to employee development, whichever method is chosen, it must be mutually agreed between you. Feedback from the employee is also vital to confirm whether the training has:

- met the needs of the individual or business;
- improved the skills of the employee;
- highlighted that other training requirements are needed.

Whenever you conduct staff appraisals, management should avoid the 'them' and 'us' situation and try not to judge the employee. To prevent this from happening, encourage staff to self-assess their performances before the appraisal. This can be difficult at first without a little help or encouragement, but it will certainly create a more constructive assessment.

An appraisal is not simply a random discussion; it must be well thought out and a two-way experience. Different types of questions have differing uses within the appraisal process, such as:

- **Open questions.** Used to begin a discussion and gain information.

- **Probing questions.** Used to discover more about a topic.

- **Closed questions.** Used to gain agreement.

- **Hypothetical questions.** Used to create imaginative thinking.

- **Confirming questions.** Used to confirm that you understand what was said.

Your expectations should be made clear to the employee during the appraisal and a written report of the meeting should be drafted and a copy handed to the employee as soon as possible after the appraisal is concluded. Every employee should be given the opportunity to respond to any concerns raised and provide mitigating evidence or explanations.

 Applaud success in public, but berate in private.

It's important to address poor performance issues as early as possible, together with the consequences, if the employee fails to improve. In these circumstances, reflect upon the possibility of arranging for a co-worker to act as a role model or mentor as this could turn a poor performing member of staff into a great one.

Managing performance

The secret of managing an employee's performance and getting the best from him is to remember that everyone is different and will have varying approaches to work. Recognising your employees as individuals and applying the correct management techniques will go a long way to maximise your efforts in building the best performing team possible for your business.

I am now going to contradict myself. Although every member of your staff is an individual, they nevertheless fall into various groupings. Being aware of those groups and the management techniques you should use is the first step in getting the best results from your team of employees. These groups are as follows: .

- **'The plodders'.** This group will produce satisfactory levels of output and will go on forever. However, they are capable of improving themselves and their performance. To improve their results:
  - set medium-term objectives that will match their ability;
  - review their performance regularly;
  - provide regular feedback and encouragement;
  - don't let them get comfortable, but ease them gently into their stretch zones.

- **'Dead wood'.** No business can afford to carry this type of group. Their performance is generally inadequate and they only survive due to poor management. Fortunately, this type of group is usually only found within the larger business as they can hide in a crowd. Dead wood must be dealt with sympathetically but firmly to try to improve their performance. If they are left alone, not only will their performance suffer, but they can also de-motivate other employees. To improve their results:
  - don't avoid confronting them, but deal with their performance;
  - identify their strengths and build upon them (remember the SWOT analysis);
  - set short-term objectives and praise success;
  - provide structured training.

- **'High-flyers'.** This group is capable, enthusiastic and always seeks a challenge. They are invaluable to a business in terms of energy and productivity, but they can be very difficult to manage. Care needs to be exercised to ensure that they stay on the straight and narrow and don't go off on a tangent and do their own thing. To improve their results:
  - make sure that the 'high-flyers' remain focused on agreed goals;
  - challenge them by setting long-term objectives;
  - delegate meaningful tasks and use their skills to the optimum level;
  - review their performance regularly and increase their stretch zone by providing suitable opportunities.

- **'Fence sitters'.** This group usually puts in a satisfactory performance, but can be influenced by external or internal factors that can stop them going that 'extra mile'. To improve their results:

  - hold regular review meetings;

  - give them short-term objectives and keep them focused;

  - find out what 'turns them on' and try to develop their role to accommodate this;

  - deal with poor performance as soon as it begins to occur or it will simply get worse.

- **'Trainees'.** This group is the future of any business and is useful as part of your business, but they can be demanding in terms of commitment. Initially, they will require guidelines along which they should operate, as well as regular feedback. To improve their results:

  - set short-term development objectives;

  - seek the aid of a 'plodder' as this will free up your time and will be good development for the 'plodder';

  - produce a coaching plan to build up their experience.

Good staff need a good leader. Unfortunately, leadership cannot be taught; you can only learn it yourself. By establishing what your own strengths and weaknesses are and by ruthlessly and objectively working over a period of time to turn the weaknesses into strengths, you can grow into a strong and resourceful leader who people will look up to and admire, There are three areas that determine the success of a leader and they are as follows:

1. **Planning** – determining how objectives will be achieved.

2. **Team building and training** – ensuring that team members are selected, trained, developed and carry out their tasks to a pre-determined standard.

3. **Performance management** – motivating and improving the performance and personal development of individual team members so that set objectives are achieved.

To be an effective manager and leader you must ensure that you are effective in all of the above three areas and that they are kept in balance. These techniques are easy to learn and not difficult to apply as they are all based on common sense and an understanding of why people do things.

 Staff loyalty can be boosted by introducing a pension scheme, but do beware as without the help of an independent pension specialist it could turn into your worst nightmare.

There are many actions that business owners and managers can take to prevent poor performance, such as setting standards of performance and explaining these to your staff, as well as induction training. In addition, the following will go a long way to alleviate the problem:

- Provide accurate job descriptions.

- Make sure that workloads are manageable and resources sufficient.

- Ensure that the needs of people with disabilities are met.

- Address the root cause and not just the symptoms of failure.

Once your first members of staff are in place and trained, this is not the end of the recruitment process. Your firm will expand and other workers may need to be employed, but before you spend time and money on a new member of staff, ask yourself if existing employees could share the extra workload. Perhaps introducing overtime may be the answer, because taking on another member of staff not only increases your wage bill, but also means he will need equipment, which costs more money.

If you are considering taking on a manager for the first time, before bringing someone new on board look at your existing employees to see if one could be promoted. This will do more for staff morale than anything else.

Disciplinary and grievance procedures

Every business must have grievance and disciplinary procedures in place and the basic information relating to these issues needs to be part of the employee's written statement or staff handbook. Spell out what is and isn't acceptable behaviour in the workplace and set down simple rules for employees to follow if they feel that they have a complaint about their treatment. This will prevent you from facing an employment tribunal and paying heavy fines.

 Employees who are suspended pending a disciplinary investigation should receive full pay unless it's stated otherwise in their statement or contract of employment.

When you are drawing up disciplinary rules that will set your standards of conduct and the grievance procedures in place, follow the ACAS code of practice. It's there to help you make sure that you deal with these issues fairly and that your employees have the opportunity to put their side of the story.

The ACAS code of practice on disciplinary and grievance procedures states that good disciplinary measures should be in writing and state to whom they apply. They must be non-discriminatory and should ensure that problems are dealt with quickly, as well as:

- ensuring that all information is kept confidential;

- stating who has the authority to take disciplinary action and the type of action that may be taken;

- ensuring that the employees are informed about the complaints against them and provided with any evidence;

- giving workers the chance to put their side of the story and allow them to have a companion at the hearing;

- not dismissing an employee for a first offence, except for gross misconduct;

- ensuring that no disciplinary action is taken before fully investigating the case;

- ensuring that the employees are given an explanation for any penalty imposed;

- informing employees that they have a right to appeal against any decision and explain the appeal procedure.

What constitutes unacceptable behaviour in your firm should be explained in such a manner so that your employee can never be in any doubt. These can include anything that can affect the smooth running of your business to the safety of fellow workers, for example:

- Absenteeism and timekeeping
- Health and safety
- Standards of work
- Personal appearance
- Use of your business's facilities (including private telephone calls and emails) without authority
- Smoking
- Discrimination

Gross misconduct is an action or series of actions so serious that you may dismiss an employee for his first offence without notice or pay in lieu of notice. However, normal practice dictates that an employee is suspended pending an investigation of the incident and is given an opportunity to put his case at a meeting.

 Minor breaches of rules should be dealt with speedily and informally.

Offences that are classed as gross misconduct and result in instant dismissal are as follows:

- Theft and fraud
- Fighting or assault
- Deliberate damage to your business property
- Being under the influence of illegal drugs or alcohol

Serious negligence of duty that leads to unacceptable loss, damage or injury, including severe acts of insubordination, also comes within the scope of gross misconduct.

Grievance procedures, on the other hand, follow along the same lines as disciplinary matters, insomuch as all businesses are required to follow the minimum guidelines as laid down in the ACAS code of practice. This allows your employees to bring their complaints about their employment to you without fear of victimisation.

 Employment policies need to be reviewed and amended where necessary on a regular basis, say at least every 12 months.

These procedures must also be in written form and must be part of either the statement, contract of employment or a staff handbook. The common stages of any grievance measures are as follows:

1. The employee informs his employer in writing of his grievance.

2. The employee is then invited to a meeting to discuss his grievance. He has the right to be accompanied by a colleague.

3. You, as the employer, respond to his complaint.

4. The employee is given the right to appeal if he feels that the grievance has not been handled satisfactorily.

While all businesses are required to have the procedures mentioned above in place, they are not there just to protect the employee but are for your benefit as well. Hopefully, you will never have to use them.

Grievance procedures play an important part in modern business structures today. For one thing, it lets your employees know that you care about their welfare and interests. If a grievance is allowed to fester and is not dealt with speedily, it could result in bad employee/employer relations, which may also develop into a major dispute and this has got to be bad for any business.

Letting people go

Letting people go is a tricky and unpleasant business at the best of times, but if you don't get it right, you could find yourself in front of an employment tribunal charged with unfair dismissal. If your ex-employee is successful in arguing his case, you or your business could be facing a substantial claim of compensation. Therefore, to be fair you must have a very good reason to sack your workers. Potentially valid reasons for letting people go will relate to:

- the employee's ability or qualifications to do the job;

- the employee's conduct;

- the employee's position being made redundant;

- any legal requirements that prevent a worker carrying out his duty (e.g. a driver is banned from driving).

Probationary periods of employment when taking on new employees are one way to circumnavigate the problem of unfair dismissal. But it's still advisable to draw up a list of reasons why you are not making the position permanent.

 Employees must lodge any claim for unfair dismissal within three months of leaving their employment.

Some dismissals are deemed automatically to be unfair. These include the following:

- Dismissing an employee or selecting him for redundancy when others in similar circumstances are not considered.

- A failure to follow basic disciplinary procedures.

- An employee is given notice on grounds of:

  - Pregnancy

  - Colour or race

  - Religion

  - Disability

  - Sexual orientation

  - Age discrimination

When dismissing people you must always show that you have acted reasonably and followed the right procedures. All employees you dismiss, other than for gross misconduct, are entitled to a minimum period of notice. The amount of notice will depend on their period of employment with you; for example, one week's notice if they have been with you for at least a month. Employees with two years' service must be given two weeks' notice. They are also entitled to a further week's notice for each further year of employment up to a maximum of 12 weeks' notice. You can, of course, include longer periods of notice within your contract of employment. You are also obliged to pay your employees their normal rates of pay during their period of notice including the minimum rate of pay if they are on sick leave, holiday or maternity leave during the period of their notice.

 Cutting someone's salary can force an employee to resign and he can still make a claim for unfair dismissal.

Redundancy, on the other hand, is an entirely different matter and usually comes about if you experience a downturn in business, or you change the way your business operates. The rules on redundancy state that if you are making more than 20 people redundant, you must consult your employees or their representative. In practice, it's advisable to consult with your staff if only one or two are being made redundant. Redundancy is defined as dismissing an employee because you are:

- closing your business;
- closing your employee's workplace;
- introducing automated equipment.

Normally the job in question would have disappeared before you consider redundancy. You will also need to take steps to avoid compulsory redundancy by considering working alternatives, such as short-time working or job sharing, early retirement or shedding temporary labour. The selection process needs to be unbiased and if you are basing it on poor performance, you should back it up with evidence from your staff appraisal system.

 You are required to pay certain minimum amounts to employees who qualify for tax-free redundancy pay when their jobs are lost. Check with www.berr.gov.uk for the current rates.

You should make available to all employees being made redundant retraining facilities and reasonable time off on full pay so that they can seek alternative employment.

There will be times when you will be asked to give a written explanation for dismissing an employee. If an employee has been in continuous employment with you for at least 12 months and makes this request either orally or in writing, you must provide a written statement setting out the reason within 14 days.

When dismissing a woman who is pregnant or who is on maternity or adoption leave, you must give her a written statement of your reasons whether she has asked for it or not, irrespective of her length of service.

Staff handbooks

Providing employees with a handbook in addition to their statement or contract of employment gives them a valuable reference manual containing important information about your business and their employment, which can be easily consulted at any time. For you, the businessperson, it can also be an aid to induction, training, communications and recruitment. As well as giving employees written information about their terms and conditions of employment, it can also be used to provide specialist information for employees of those businesses who have staff working at home, or those working alone who travel and visit homes or other places at unsociable hours. Other policies that may be included in a staff handbook could be:

- Whistleblowing policies
- Harassment policies
- Reporting procedures

These are, of course, additional to the terms and conditions that are normally to be found in contracts of employment.

 Highlight those parts of the handbook containing employees' terms and conditions.

Using and bringing together existing material means a handbook can easily be produced. Take care with the layout and presentation to ensure that the contents are clear and can be understood by using simple language and avoiding pompous and legalistic jargon.

It's always advisable to break up the text by using charts, graphs and illustrations to make your handbook user friendly.

Finally, use the opening pages of your handbook to provide new employees with information about your business, its organisation and products or services.

Take heed

Employee rights are protected when a business is sold or transferred

The new owner cannot change the terms of employment without the employee's consent

---

CHAPTER 6

Being in control

What you'll find in this chapter

- ✔ Survival income
- ✔ Cash flow forecasting
- ✔ Profit and loss forecasting
- ✔ Understanding book-keeping
- ✔ Sales ledger management
- ✔ Summing up your finances
- ✔ Knowing your business
- ✔ Data protection

To determine the success of your business, you will need to put in place some financial targets against which you can measure your performance. This means attempting to predict levels of income and expenditure. After you have commenced trading, review the achievement of your business against these targets. Not only will this review tell you if you are successful, but also it will highlight any problems, rising costs or customers who consistently pay too late, for instance, and will monitor your incoming money. You must keep track of your expenditure, however. It will be difficult to know where you stand if you are lacking any form of fiscal information.

Forecasting your cash flow requirements over the first 12 months and extending this prognosis into the next two to three years will tell you if you need to raise external finance for your business and if so, how much. It's important to update these forecasts on a regular basis. Initially, you can only estimate your requirements, but when trading commences you will be in a position to predict your future needs more accurately.

 Working capital is the term used to describe the finance used by businesses for everyday trading purposes.

When calculating how much money is needed to set up your business you must take into account the loss of earnings you will suffer. The everyday expenditure of your private life will not go away. Therefore, it's time to look at your personal requirements. After all, one of the main reasons for going into business for yourself was to improve your overall standard of living!

 If you don't know how much money is owed to you or by you, you could lose control of the business you worked so hard to create.

Survival income

In general, you would expect your business to make much more money than is necessary to cover the financial demands of everyday private life. Initially, it may take time for your business to generate sufficient turnover to meet the expenditure of the business as well as your income. Therefore, it's essential that you don't withdraw excessive amounts to live on. It's useful to know the minimum amount of money you will need to take out of the business to meet all of your personal expenses over a given period. This is called 'survival income'.

 When planning survival income always consider a fail-safe element to cover unforeseen occurrences, such as a washing machine breaking down.

To determine survival income, you need to establish who makes up your family unit or the number of people who are dependent upon your income. A typical survival budget must also include any income coming into the household, including income from your spouse/partner, investments or pensions. The resulting total of expenditure over income represents your survival requirements. All items in your forecast should appear net of tax.

Sample survival income budget

Survival Income Budget

For   **Period**   **£**

Mortgage/rent _____

Council Tax/water rates _____

Fuel (gas/electric, etc.)_____

Telephone _____

Insurance (property/contents) _____

Housekeeping (food, cleaning, etc.)_____

TV licence/newspapers/trade magazines ___

Hire purchase/rental payments _____

Road tax and insurance (motor vehicles) ___

Running expenses (petrol, parking, service) ___

Fares/taxis _____

Clothing _____

Children's expenses (pocket money, etc.)___

Holidays/Christmas/birthdays _____

Life insurance/pensions _____

National Insurance _____

Pets (food, vet's bills) _____

Contingencies _____

Total expenditure:

Non-business income _____

Family/partner _____

Investments/pensions _____

Other (please specify) _____

Total income:

SURVIVAL INCOME REQUIREMENTS: £
(income less expenditure)

You also need to determine a timescale over which your survival budget will run. Although this is usually done over a year, some people find it easier to work on a monthly basis. There are four segments to a regular budget and these are usually classified as:

- Domestic expenses, such as rent or mortgage, etc.
- Travel and transport costs
- Personal expenditure, such as clothing, professional membership fees
- Non-business income

The survival income budget form, shown on the previous page, is for you to use.

 Be realistic in your survival forecasts. The higher the survival income, the more money you will need to take out of the business.

Cash flow forecasting

There are some very notable differences between forecasting profit and cash flow. The profit estimates show the gain likely to be made in any given time span. It answers the fundamental question Will the business be viable? The cash flow conjecture shows the planned dates of the movement of money either in or out of the business.

 Cash is the lifeblood of every business. Without it, your firm would not be able to operate and flourish.

A number of items shown in your cash flow forecast will be identical to those in the profit forecast, although they will be dealt with in a different manner. For example, sales made in June will be invoiced and shown in the June figures. But if they were not paid until two months later, the receipts will be registered in the August cash flow forecasts. This principle also applies to your purchases. For VAT-registered businesses, VAT is not a profit and loss item.

Sample cash flow forecast guide

CASH FLOW FORECAST GUIDE

For DWR Software
PERIOD June 2008 to May 2009

RECEIPTS	Month: June		Month: July	
	Budget	Actual	Budget	Actual
Cash sales		500	2,000	2,000
Cash from debtors			10,000	11,000
Capital introduced	5,000	5,000		
Total receipts (a)	**5,000**	**5,500**	**12,000**	**13,000**
PAYMENTS				
For goods received	2,100	2,400	9,700	14,800
Salaries/National Insurance	650	900	1,800	2,100
Rent/rates	150	150		
Insurance	350	350		
Repair & renewals				
Heating/light/power			325	475
Postage/printing/stationery	1,000	1,200		
Car/travelling				60
Telephone			210	290
Professional fees				
Capital payments	1,000	2,450	1,000	1,000
Interest charges	75	150	150	200
VAT payable (refund)				
Drawings			1,500	1,250
Total payments (b)	**5,325**	**7,600**	**14,685**	**20,175**
Net cash flow (a – b)	**(325)**	**(2,100)**	**(2,685)**	**(7,175)**
Opening balance			(325)	(2,100)
Closing balance	(325)	(2,100)	(3,010)	(9,275)

It will, however, appear in your cash flow forecasts. Receipts that are not profit and loss items include:

- Loans
- Money invested by the owners
- Capital expenditure

However, the dates these items are due in or out are to be included in the cash flow forecast. Conversely, depreciation is a profit and loss cost to the business but doesn't appear in the cash flow reports.

Seeing your income and expenditure itemised in this manner gives you a clear idea of budgetary requirements. Note that the terms on which you trade will have a direct effect on the cash flow of your business.

The headings of the model on the previous page may differ according to the requirements of your business. From this example you will see arrangements for an additional cash injection will need to be made; perhaps a loan from your bank or other lender would be a viable option.

 Having enough cash to pay creditors, wages, and other bills as they fall due is vital to your business survival.

Notes on the cash flow forecast

- **Receipts:** the money coming into your business. This will be mainly from sales once your business is established.
- **Payments:** all the money going out of your business. It will include payments to your supplier and capital or rental payments for cars or other equipment needed to run your business. All cash flow payments and receipts will be inclusive of VAT where applicable.

The term 'working capital' is used to describe the day-to-day financial resources used by your business for everyday trading purposes. They consist of:

- **Debtors:** customers to whom you have sold your goods or services on credit and who owe you money.

- **Cash:** the amount of money you have in your till, or deposited in your bank account.

- **Creditors:** the people you have bought from and now owe the price of your purchases.

- **Stock:** the value of materials purchased for resale, or materials to be transformed into finished objects.

Working capital needs to be carefully controlled so that your enterprise can flourish.

Collecting the money due to you on time is important. Every day a customer delays payment your profit margins are eroded, because of the time delay between the purchase of your materials, the time when they are sold and the time the cash is actually received. Such a delay usually leads to a cash flow shortfall, a situation that can affect even those profitable businesses with full order books. It's vital to have enough cash at your disposal to meet these eventualities and thereby avoid the pitfalls of over-trading.

 A word of caution about over-trading; a common but unfortunate occurrence for many developing businesses. While sales are an indispensable requisite, a sudden increase can be dangerous, since the more sales you make, the more money you need to purchase materials to support those sales.

Profit and loss forecasting

This forecast should contain information on your income and expenditure, similar to the previous forecast, except that the emphasis is on the profitability of your business. Forecasts usually cover a 12-month period, but can be set at shorter intervals provided that they are eventually collated to produce a yearly one. For periods exceeding a year, you will need to complete a forecast for each annual period.

Sample profit and loss forecast guide

PROFIT & LOSS FORECAST GUIDE

For DWR Software

PERIOD June 2008 to May 2009

RECEIPTS	Month: June		Month: July	
	Budget	**Actual**	**Budget**	**Actual**
Sales (net of VAT) (a)	14,500	12,250	16,500	17,000
Less direct costs:				
Cost of materials	9,450	8,150	10,750	11,000
Cost of sales (advertising)	800	750	1,000	975
Gross profit (b)	**4,250**	**3,350**	**4,750**	**5,025**
Gross profit margin (b/a x 100%)	**29.3%**	**27.3%**	**28.8%**	**29.5%**
Overheads:				
Salaries/National Insurance	750	950	1,800	2,100
Rent/rates	150	150		
Insurance	75	80		
Repairs & renewals			250	100
Heating/light/power			325	475
Postage/printing/stationery	1,000	600		
Car/travelling				60
Telephone		85	100	140
Professional fees	400	400		
Interest charges	75	110	150	200
Total overheads (c)	**2,450**	**2,375**	**2,625**	**3,075**
Trading profit (b) – (c)	1,800	975	2,125	1,950
Less depreciation	150	125	150	125
Net profit before tax	**1,650**	**850**	**1,975**	**1,825**
Cumulative net profit			3,625	2,675

'Income 20 shillings, expenditure 19 shillings and six pence – result – happiness.

Income 20 shillings, expenditure 20 shillings and six pence – result – misery.'

(Mr Micawber)

It's advisable to show items of expenditure in the months they were incurred. For example, rent for your business premises may only be paid quarterly. However, each quarterly payment represents rent for each month you occupy the building. Therefore, each quarterly bill should be divided by a third and allocated to each month of that quarter. The same procedure applies to telephone accounts and other similar items. The item of depreciation in the profit and loss forecast guide (see opposite) is a means of spreading the cost of machinery, vehicles and other assets over the span of their useful lives.

For those of you who will be VAT registered, Value Added Tax (VAT) doesn't need to be included in your profit and loss forecast. Normally, it doesn't constitute a cost to your business.

If you expect to increase your sales, you must consider the effect this will have on the amount of working capital you will need. However, it should be included in your cash flow forecast. Profit and loss forecasts for your business plan normally take a complete overview of your business. Nevertheless, forecasts can be made on each product or service you offer. This will allow you to discard any unprofitable segment of your business.

TIP Careful forecasting will help you to avoid any unexpected and harmful surprises.

To keep the above specimen as uncomplicated as possible 'work in progress' has been omitted. 'Work in progress' is the term used to describe the value of work or stock in hand that has been completed but not sold. In some businesses, particularly in building and manufacturing, it can be an important part of the profit and loss forecast. This forecast can be adjusted for 'stock' or 'work in progress' by adding to the cost of materials the difference between the value at the beginning and at end of the period. This item should always be accounted for at cost. Your accountant can supply further advice on this topic.

A proportion of your home rent or mortgage, as well as services such as gas and electricity, can be included if you work from home.

Notes on the profit and loss forecast

The definition of sales can be given as the value of stock sold and invoiced, regardless of whether payment has been received or not. Cost of materials is the actual cost, to you, of what you sell – whether you have paid for these items is not relevant. However, this cost of materials doesn't include one-off purchases such as a computer, nor would it appear elsewhere in this forecast, because it's regarded as part of your business's assets.

 Review your firm's overheads on a regular basis. Always look for ways to reduce costs.

Overheads will vary from business to business. If you are renting separate business premises, your rent, plus the cost of rates and other expenses, is to be included in your profit and loss report.

Understanding book-keeping

Although items in this section will not be used in your business plan, it's important to have a fundamental understanding of the subject. In the UK you are legally obligated to keep accurate records of all your business activities. An efficient system is an essential part of any well-run business. You will find it an indispensable aid in keeping your firm's finances under control.

An ideal book-keeping system for new or small businesses is to be found in Lawpack's *Book-Keeping Made Easy*. The book starts you off with a basic method of recording all your business transactions, and then takes you into the double-entry methods as your business expands. Furthermore, it explains how to use the information stored within your financial records to your advantage.

Before you commence trading, you should take advantage of the book-keeping seminars organised by your local small business centre, particularly if your book-keeping experience is limited.

If you have a computer, there are also many software packages available. In this section we will only deal with the cash book and purchase ledger; the sales ledger and information about credit control are being handled separately later in this chapter.

Maintaining accurate records will help you in many ways. Not only will you be able to meet your legal obligations, but you will also find it easier to complete your returns to HM Revenue & Customs (HMRC) for Income Tax purposes, not to mention your submissions for VAT.

 Always keep private money separate from the cash in your business.

You will also need to take data from these records to update your cash flow and profit and loss figures. By exercising control over your finances, you can reduce the workload of your accountant, which in turn will help him to reduce his bills.

 Justifiable records are essential if you are going to monitor your performance and control your cash flow.

It's not difficult to keep accurate records, nor should it be time-consuming. At first, all you may need is a few folders in which you will need to retain:

- sales invoices to your customers (if retailing, cash or till receipts);
- purchase invoices from your suppliers;
- bank statements;
- petty cash receipts and purchase slips.

 Don't forget your firm's petty cash is not to be treated as your personal pocket money.

This system will help you to keep everything in order and up to date. It will prove important when you go to the next stage and introduce book-keeping into the business. These records not only will allow you to keep track of the money coming in and going out, but also will provide instant information on how well you are doing financially.

 In theory, the entries in your cash book should mirror the items in your bank statement. You will need to reconcile both against each other, making sure you can account for any difference.

The cash book is the most important book for you to keep. It summarises your daily receipts and payments, and contains the method of payment and names of the parties concerned with each transaction. These transactions can be cash, cheque, standing order, direct debit or credit card. The left-hand pages of your cash book will record money coming in – sales, while the right-hand pages will show the money you paid out – your purchases.

SAMPLE CASH BOOK – RECEIPTS

Date (1)	Customer (2)	Item (3)	Bank (4)	Cash (5)
09.06.08	A. Greendale	Invoice 2103	450.00	
12.06.08	Revenue & Customs	Tax rebate	150.00	
18.06.08	D. Bird	Sale of van	1750.00	
22.06.08	J. Bond	Invoice 2098		38.46
27.06.08	P. Sterling	Deposit		250.00
02.07.08	M. Cash	Invoice 2104	850.00	

Column (1) records the date of when the cheque or cash was received. Columns (2) and (3) note the name of the customer paying you and the reason for the payment. The remaining columns denote whether or not the money has been banked or taken into petty cash.

Now let us look at the payment side of your cash book.

The items marked (1) to (5) record the movement of outgoing cash from your business, stating date, supplier and method of payment. The remaining columns provide an analysis of the types of expenses you are incurring. The number of columns required will depend on the nature of your business.

SAMPLE CASH BOOK – PAYMENTS

Date (1)	Supplier (2)	Item (3)	Bank (4)	Cash (5)	Materials	Wages/NI	Rent	Elec	Print	Phone	Trav
02.06.08	Br Tel	Chq 321	200							200	
05.06.08	Reed Gar	Fuel		35							35
12.06.08	P.O.	Stamps	15							15	
14.06.08	Sharp & Co	Chq 322	174							174	
18.06.08	HH Prop	D/D	380				380				
29.06.08	D.Boy	Chq 323	865.45		865.45						

 Employing a book-keeper, on either a full- or part-time basis, need not cost the earth. It will, however, leave you free to manage your business and avoid stress.

A purchase or bought ledger book will deal with all your purchases. It's advisable to have two folders – one for purchases paid and another for those unpaid. To simplify matters, a separate page should be used for each supplier. With this record book you can see at a glance what materials you purchase and whether or not you have paid for the goods in question.

 Paying your suppliers on time creates good business relationships. It will also ensure that you always get good service.

Each bought ledger account should be headed with the supplier's name, address and telephone number. Always include the name of your contact and the credit limit you have been granted. On the right-hand side enter details of all your purchases, along with:

- your order number;
- the date of the order;
- special instructions (if any);
- the agreed delivery date.

On the left-hand side of the account you must record each payment you make, noting the date and cheque number.

 Knowing exactly how much you owe and when it's due at any particular time will check any overspending.

Total both columns each month. Subtract the amount you have paid from your total purchases. The sum remaining should reconcile with your supplier's statement. To keep track of your purchases, always ensure that you receive an invoice for your purchases and a receipt for any payments. Invoices should be kept in an unpaid folder in date order. When you send a cheque in payment of an invoice, note the date and cheque number on the invoice, in case of any future query. Now place the invoice in the invoices paid folder.

 The manner in which you deal with your bought and sales ledgers should not differ. The only distinction is that one records what you owe, the other what is due to you.

Sales ledger management

If you are a retailer dealing mainly with cash, a sales ledger will be of little use to you. However, you will need to keep a summary of daily sales. Your cash book, described earlier, can be easily adapted for this purpose. For many businesses, the sales ledger will be the most valuable asset – so manage it with care!

Your sales ledger will be arranged in exactly the same way as your purchase ledger, with one account per customer. The main difference between the two is that the sales ledger should contain the name of the person who pays your account, the name and position of the individual who accepts your deliveries, and the person who checks your invoice. This saves time when you need to chase for any outstanding sums due.

 To save time and money every month, don't send statements of account to customers with a zero balance. Send the remainder by first-class post.

All sales should be recorded on the left-hand side of your ledger, and all payments received on the right. At the end of each month, add up each column by subtracting the money received from the sales. This will

PENNY STERLING TOYS

Unit 5, Nonsuch Industrial Estate
Anytown Road,
Anytown WW11 XX22

Tel: 0000 000 000
Fax: 0000 000 001

Invoice No: 123456   **Date:** 7 November 2008

To:

1 Box	12 assorted jigsaw puzzles @ £1.25p each	15.00
3 Dozen	Yo-yos @ £9 per dozen	27.00
4 Each	Playstations® @ £125.60 each	502.40
Subtotal:		544.40
VAT @ 17.5%		95.27
Total:		639.67

Credit Terms: 30 days from the date of invoice

VAT Registration No: 987 6543 21

determine how much you are owed by each customer. A statement detailing the items sold to the customer and payments received should be sent each month to every customer, but before doing so you should check that your balances agree.

To help you keep control of your sales, always issue an invoice. Invoices should be numbered in sequence and a copy retained for your folder. Copies of your customers' invoices should be kept in sales paid and unpaid folders, to be dealt with in the same manner as outlined in the purchase ledger section. Your terms of trade should be clearly displayed on all communications to your customers, thus avoiding any misunderstanding about when you expect to be paid.

> If a customer queries an order or invoice, always treat that complaint with urgency. Outstanding problems such as these are the most common reason for non-payment of an account.

Keep a regular check on your unpaid invoices. Any overdue accounts should be chased persistently but politely. When contacting customers about unpaid accounts, always chase those customers who owe the largest amounts first. If you keep a routine check on outstanding sums due, you won't need to worry quite so much about its age.

> Never be afraid to ask your customer for the money owed to you. Otherwise, he will use you as a source of interest-free credit.

While it may not be possible for you to telephone all your customers each month to collect the money due to you, direct telephone contact is the best method to use, particularly for your larger accounts. The smaller accounts should be contacted by a cycle of three or four letters, starting with a gentle reminder and finishing with a serious demand for payment. However, for the best effect, this letter cycle should be varied, or your customer will soon learn to delay payment until the final demand.

> In an average business, 80 per cent of outstanding debt is owed by only 20 per cent of its customers. Chasing larger debts first improves your cash flow.

Late payment can have a devastating effect on the liquidity of small and start-up businesses, so don't let your customers acquire the habit of late payment. Persistent and friendly reminders, preferably by telephone as soon as or before payment is due, should do the trick. If that doesn't work, you have the legal right to claim interest on the overdue amount if it's another business paying you late, unless your invoices or terms of trade say otherwise.

The rate of interest you are able to charge is calculated at the Bank of England base rate plus eight per cent. So if the base rate is four per cent, you can charge your late-paying customers 12 per cent. The rates for calculating interest are fixed in six-monthly periods. The base rate at 31 December is used for debts becoming late between January and June. The rate in force on 30 June will be applicable for the next six months. VAT is unaffected as you can claim on the full amount of the debt including VAT, but VAT is not levied on the interest you claim. In addition, you can also claim for reasonable debt recovery costs including court fees.

To claim interest from wayward customers you should:

- notify the customer in writing of your plans;

- contact habitual late payers to explain how they will be affected and ensure that they understand your payment terms;

- ensure that all invoices show the date when payment is due;

- state that you reserve the right to charge interest on invoices and other documents bearing your terms of trade, even if you don't intend to do so;

- present your late-paying customers with a statement showing that the original sum and interest has been paid, and outlining the interest received.

Never forget that your suppliers are entitled to charge the same interest rates if you fail to pay their accounts as they become due.

Within your sales ledger operation there should be an element of credit management. The aim of credit control is to eliminate the risk of bad debt as much as possible. Controlling credit also means obtaining bank and business references not only from new customers, but also from existing ones, at regular intervals. Beware – your customers' financial standing can change overnight, and it won't necessarily be a change for the better!

> **TIP** Always check out a customer's potential ability to pay before granting credit.

In addition, do ensure that your book-keeping system enables you to issue invoices promptly and indicates when they become overdue. Here are some other helpful hints:

- Clearly set out your terms of trading and don't deviate from them. Make sure that customers are aware of these terms. Notify them of any changes the instant that they occur.

- Keep clear and precise records. If you keep inaccurate accounts or invoices, your customers will have an excuse to delay paying you.

- Collect payments on time by establishing a collection pattern and sticking to it.

- If a customer promises to put a cheque in the post and it doesn't arrive, chase him for it again.

- If routine chasing doesn't produce results, stop further supplies to that customer as soon as it's viable to do so. Moreover, use the services of a reputable collection agency to resolve the situation.

Summing up your finances

Having absolute control of your finances testifies to others that you are committed to the ultimate success of your business and lets them know that you can be relied upon to conduct your business in a professional manner. By making certain that you will be paid on time, you ensure that you have the cash to expand and enjoy your newly-found prosperity.

Knowing your business

From the moment your business begins to trade, you start to collect information about your customers, the type of goods or services they purchase, cash flow and budgets. These are just a few of the many items of information that will be scattered around your business. The problem is collating this data and using it wisely.

The financial information will be found within the book-keeping and accounting methods discussed earlier in this chapter. Other intelligence sources will be located within your:

- **sales invoices:** these will tell you who is buying what, when and why;

- **purchase orders:** these will tell you what your suppliers are charging you and their level of service;

- **customer complaints:** these will let you know what your customers think of your products or service.

One of the most reliable sources of information about your business should come to light if you hold open and frank staff appraisals. The feedback from these will be invaluable to you.

Gathering all the information you can about your business, staff and its customers will give you more control. Furthermore, checking the progress of your business on a monthly basis will allow you to anticipate problems before they arise and resolve them before they can do any harm. In other words, your business will remain sustainable.

A regular review of the information within your firm will reduce business risks and personal liabilities.

Producing good management reports at regular monthly intervals will not mean lots of extra work. It's simply a matter of formalising a simple system to make sure that the key pieces of information are used effectively.

To ensure that your staff collect the information that is important to you at either weekly or monthly periods, distributing a chart on the following lines will go a long way to ensure that every bit of information is at your fingertips when you want it:

Information Required	Where From	Who Collects and Reports	Frequency
Debts	Sales ledger	R Hedges	Monthly

When checking your cash flow forecasts against variances, questions will be raised such as, 'Why did we spend more on stationery this month?' The answer to this question will enable you to keep a control of your spending.

 Only collect information that is vital to the success of your business.

Analysing where the money comes from will pinpoint which products or services are selling and those which are not. This, in turn, will let you know if you should:

- increase your marketing for that product or service;
- change the product or service to suit more customers;
- withdraw it from sale;
- develop new products or introduce additional services.

The benefits of this type of system will mean that you should never have more questions than answers, especially if you ensure that your information system is tailored to your business. Using management information will let investors, bank managers and employees know that you are in full control of your business and that it's not the other way around. This will generate confidence in your business and motivate employees.

Good use of the management information you will gather provides a summary of the current state of your business, letting you see at a glance how it's performing. Never be fooled into thinking that your annual accounts and balance sheet will provide an accurate picture of the state of your business. Audited accounts only mirror the financial state of a business on the day they are audited. The next day transactions will take place and the accounts will change – three or four months further on and your business could be in trouble. You need to be aware of pending problems to be in a position to act before they become really serious.

This is the major advantage small businesses have over their larger rivals – they can spot downturns in trade and react to them instantly.

Data protection

Having information and using it to advance your business is one thing, but information in paper or electronic form about customers, employees, suppliers or other business contacts is covered by law.

The Data Protection Act covers the processing of any personal information, which means obtaining, holding, retrieving or disclosing what is held on computers and certain manual filing systems. This also applies to erasing or destroying the information held. If you are processing information using computers, you have to notify the Information Commissioner of the information you are collecting and the reason why you are gathering it. An annual notification fee can be charged; for the current rate, please contact the Information Commissioner's office.

There are many businesses that don't need to notify the Commissioner. You will be exempt if you only process personal information for a limited number of business activities, such as:

- staff administration;

- advertising and marketing your products or services – this also applies if you buy in information for this purpose;

- accounting records – including information on past, existing and potential customers and suppliers which helps you make decisions on whether or not you wish to trade with them. This excludes data obtained from a credit reference agency.

You still need to comply with the Act even though you are exempt from notifying the Commissioner. The Data Protection Act is presented in a series of principles; a full list of these are available on the Commissioner's website at www.ico.gov.uk.

 To comply with the principles of the Data Protection Act, you will need to work out exactly what information you need and only collect that amount of information.

It's your duty to keep all information up to date and if an individual tells you that his information is inaccurate, you must correct it within 28 days.

Make sure that your information storage systems are secure and that your staff are trained in good information handling practices.

You can also provide individuals with information you hold on them if they make a request in writing. You are able to charge them £10 for providing this information in an understandable format and it must be delivered to them within 40 days of them making a request.

You are not allowed to transfer information outside the European Economic Area unless you are sure that the country has adequate data protection laws or you have the individual's consent.

CHAPTER 7

Funding your business

What you'll find in this chapter

✔ How much do you really need?
✔ Where to raise capital
✔ Unconventional financing
✔ Grants and the Small Firms Loan Guarantee scheme
✔ Analysing your business funding

Traditionally, new businesses that need extra funding turn to the bank for an overdraft, forgetting that this arrangement is suitable only for short-term use. Instead, new businesses should be planning to use the medium-to long-term finance facilities that are really needed to get started. When borrowing money as a new business, you must be well prepared before approaching a potential lender – no matter what type of financial injection you are seeking for your business. Do you know at this stage what most lenders are looking for when they contemplate making an advance? You should. The main factors are:

- **The owners.** Are they seen as credible, capable, competent and honest? Do they communicate effectively? Do they have a good track record in terms of employment, financial/business history? Do they have the skills, knowledge, experience and the right attitudes to make the business successful?

- **Business plan.** Do they have a sound business idea? Are their forecasts reasonable, well thought out and presented in a professional manner?

> The golden rule when borrowing money to start your business is 'find your market, then the money will follow'.

- **Owners' financial investment.** How much of their own money are the owners putting into the business compared to the amount they wish to raise as loans? Depending on the economic climate and type of business, most banks prefer not to lend more than 50 per cent of the total capital required, although this percentage may be increased due to government guarantees. These are dealt with later in this chapter. Don't fret if you haven't sufficient private funds to meet 50 per cent of the investment – go to the section on government grants discussed later in this chapter.

- **Security.** It's easier to raise money and obtain a higher borrowing ratio if you have something of value to pledge against the loan. Preferred securities are those that can quickly be converted into cash in the event of default. Quoted shares, premium bonds, endowment policies and property that can be sold at auction are all considered as suitable security for loan purposes. Bear in mind that your security – your home, if used – is at risk if you fail to meet the terms of the loan.

To help you estimate the value of your personal assets, use the template 'Estimate of personal wealth' on the following page.

It's essential to build a firm, friendly alliance with your lenders. As most high-street banks have business advisers to assist you in setting up your bank account, it shouldn't be too difficult to find one of these with whom you may develop a more complex relationship. By working together, you can tackle challenges as they arise and resolve potentially difficult situations before they become problems. Any foreseeable difficulties on the horizon could affect the way you meet your obligations, so tell your lender in advance, not when it's too late. Provided you keep your lender informed on a regular basis, telling him of good times as well as bad, you should find that he willingly listens and gladly assists you through any difficult patches you encounter.

> Work out exactly the amount you want to borrow, why you want it and how you will repay it.

Estimate of personal wealth template

Property	
Value of house	
Value of other property	
Savings/Insurance	
Surrender value of insurance policies	
Cash in bank/on deposit	
Other Assets	
Value of car(s)	
Other	
Realisable assets (things you could sell to raise money)	
TOTAL ASSETS	
Liabilities	
Outstanding mortgage	
Other outstanding loans	
TOTAL CURRENT LIABILITIES	
ESTIMATED NET ASSETS (Total assets less total liabilities)	

How much do you really need?

The amount you need to borrow depends on the shortfall you discovered when you produced your cash flow forecast. Deciding on the amount of money you will need to purchase equipment or premises is fairly easy. Determining the amount of money you will need to cover gaps between your income and expenditure is a little more difficult. However, you don't have to rely on one finance house or bank. Each institution has facilities to meet different requirements, so perhaps a combination of lenders will prove right for you.

 The greater the depth of your market research, the more reliable your figures will be.

Although your forecast would have taken your projected sales and the trading terms of both your business and your suppliers into the equation, these figures are only estimates until you actually start trading. Slightly overestimating your financial requirements must be better than having to go back to your banker, cap in hand, to ask for more cash within a short period of time. All lenders frown when this happens, as they wonder what else you have hidden from them or just consider that you are poor at planning your financial requirements. Either way it will not help your cause.

Along with calculating the right amount of cash you need to borrow, you will need to decide upon the right length of time for repaying any advance. A carefully construed cash flow plan will point out the peaks and troughs of your incoming and outgoing cash and answer this question.

 When calculating the length of time you wish to repay the loan, don't forget to take into account seasonal sales patterns, such as Christmas.

Should a bank or other potential lender turn down your application for a loan, always ask why. It could be something trivial you overlooked in your business plan that can be adjusted before you approach another lender.

Where to raise capital

Again, the answer to this question depends on why you want the finance, so let's take a look at the varying financial institutions which are just waiting to lend you money.

- **High-street banks.** These, including ex-building societies, which also have a commercial lending department, are normally the first port of call. The finance they offer embraces:

    - *Overdrafts.* These are mainly short-term loans designed to provide stopgap funds to meet an unexpected shortfall, but are definitely not suitable as a replacement for long-term capital. The main disadvantage is that the overdraft may have to be repaid on demand, so reliance on them should be avoided for anything other than short-term use.

    - *Credit cards.* While not an ideal way to finance your business, they can be useful for covering temporary cash flow problems. They would cover urgent stock purchase when faced with a sudden rush of sales, for instance. If you repay the facility when your account is received, the loan will be interest free, but prohibitive interest charges make the credit card unsuitable for long-term use.

    - *Loans.* These can provide long-term working capital since they offer a suitable way to finance vehicles or other equipment. With a fixed-rate loan, you will know what your repayments will be each month.

    - *Mortgages.* Suitable for the purchase of freehold or long leasehold business premises, it's unlikely that a start-up business will want to take on this sort of commitment in its embryo stage. Banks do offer other types of facilities through their subsidiary companies, therefore it's advisable to check with your local branch before committing yourself.

 Before asking your bank for an overdraft to finance extra stock for a busy period such as Christmas, check with your suppliers. Some toy manufacturers, for example, offer extended credit in the run up to the holiday.

- **Finance houses.** Finance houses supply businesses with hire purchase and contract rental agreements to acquire the use of vehicles and other equipment. The use of hire purchase finance may be diminishing, but finance houses are replacing it with personal loans and contract purchase agreements. Factoring and discount houses provide off-balance-sheet finance for new and expanding businesses. They also supply finance for stock and raw materials as well as providing credit insurance.

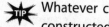 Whatever choice of finance you consider right for you, a well-constructed business plan is the only way to get it.

- **Venture capital firms.** While the principal aim of these firms is to provide start-up capital, they tend only to consider established businesses. Although the current government has expressed its concern over this practice, most of the lending in this sector has been concentrated on management buy-ins and buy-outs. To obtain finance from this source, your business must be trading as a limited company.

 Some businesses start and prosper without needing to borrow money, but most need financial help in one form or another.

- **Business angels.** These are people with some business experience who want to invest in new firms and are prepared to take greater risks than normal financiers. The level of involvement these angels offer ranges from straightforward advice to the undertaking of non-executive directorships. While it's possible to have two or three business angels investing in one business, you should agree the level of commitment from the outset of negotiations. The British Business Angels Association will direct you to local and appropriate business angel networks at www.bbaa.org.uk.

- **The Prince's Trust.** In some cases, the trust will provide funds for young people, in addition to providing training, marketing support, counselling and advice. More details of the trust can be found in chapter 9.

- **Credit unions** are springing up throughout the country, and the fact unbeknown to many is that they offer micro/small business loans.

Their maximum advance is restricted to £5,000 and repayment can be spread over three years – a handy sum for people starting out who need that little bit of extra cash to get their businesses off the ground. For contact details, check your local telephone directory.

- **The Community Development Finance Association** offers access to start-up and expansion finance through its list of members, who provide capital to individuals and organisations to create wealth in disadvantaged communities or underdeveloped markets. It can be contacted at www.cdfa.org.uk.

- **Friends and family.** Approaching your family or friends for funding can be an easy and flexible route to raising money as they are more likely to offer you favourable terms than conventional lenders. However, the downside is that your business may not be a success. A business plan will still be required and if you have been turned down by a lender, your relative needs to be told the reason. In case problems arise, you must tell him of the risks involved and present him with a worst-case scenario. Do seek professional advice before taking this route and have a formal agreement drawn up.

Unconventional financing

In your everyday life, you have probably come across bank and finance house loans, overdrafts, mortgages and hire purchase, so there is no need to discuss these matters further here. We shall go into a little more detail on leasing, factoring and stock financing, however, in order to help you learn about the right finance package for your enterprise. The financing discussed in this section will supplement any other form of borrowing you agree upon, but will not affect any overdraft or other loan arrangements you may have made.

 For businesses buying goods from abroad, you will need a letter of credit to avoid paying for goods before they are shipped. These letters of credit are issued by banks and are an internationally agreed method of payment.

What a factor can do for you

There are two methods of factoring. The first, called 'invoice factoring', directly improves your cash flow. Instead of waiting the standard 30 days or more, money will be immediately advanced to you by a factor against the value of your invoices. Normally up to 80 per cent, this figure is negotiable. The factor will then take over the management of your sales ledger collections. The other 20 per cent (less the factoring fee and interest) is paid at agreed intervals. Invoice factors offer bad debt protection by way of non-recourse deals, but at a price. Your forecasts will need to project sales of about £500,000 plus.

Some invoice factors augment their services by offering stock finance, which involves securing the value of your business stock. In doing so, they can advance up to 100 per cent of your suppliers' invoices, so you benefit from any special discounts on offer.

The second method is invoice discounting, which differs from the invoice factoring option in one major way. With the discounting option, you will retain the management of your sales ledger and the responsibility for collections, so if a customer doesn't pay or goes bust, you will have to reimburse the factor. These are mainly recourse deals.

What leasing or contract hire can do for you

Principally, by using one of these options, you are given use of vehicles and equipment without having to tie up your capital. Although ownership of the equipment or motor vehicle remains with the finance house, rentals are tax-deductible items – a distinct advantage. Clearly this option is a sensible method of financing for budgetary purposes. Contract hire is best used for vehicles, since maintenance agreements can be built in. Rentals are kept low because the finance houses can reclaim the VAT levied at the time of purchase.

These types of finance have been classified as unconventional because they don't have to be listed in a firm's accounts.

At the end of a lease contract the vehicle or equipment rented must be returned to the leasing company. These items cannot be retained by the hirer.

Finance for the small exporter

All major clearing banks in the UK operate small exporter finance schemes. Conveniently, they will not interfere with any other loan or financial arrangement you have put in place. The banks provide small businesses with cash at the time an export order is shipped, provided the correct export documentation has been lodged. Banks will advance up to 100 per cent of the invoice value, less interest and a transaction fee. All small exporter programmes require adequate credit insurance cover. Therefore, if your customer doesn't pay, you will not be required to reimburse the bank. All banks carry block insurance cover arrangements, so you are saved from searching for suitable cover. Having credit insurance means lower interest charges for you.

Two other forms of non-recourse financing which are available to exporters and importers are as follows:

- **'Forfaiting'** involves bills of exchange, promissory notes or deferred letters of credit. In laypeople's terms, all of these are forms of IOUs. You discount these instruments to a forfaiting company and the risk of non-payment passes to it. Because these bills vary between 90 and 180 days, it's not unknown for them to pass from one forfaiting company to another. Forfaiting is for exporting use.

- **'Avalising'** is a simple form of a bill of exchange, allowing you to import goods from an overseas supplier on extended credit terms not normally on offer. Avalising is a form of guarantee; to 'aval' is to endorse a bill of exchange or promissory note. If the term 'Bills of Exchange' appears confusing, don't worry, it's only a document that promises to pay the named recipient an agreed sum of money on a certain date, like a cheque. Should you commence exporting at any time, go along to your local bank; it will gladly explain the procedures.

The discounting charges in respect of forfaiting and avalising must be included in your pricing policy (see chapter 2). This also covers the costs for using the small exporter schemes.

Grants and the Small Firms Loan Guarantee scheme

There are plenty of grants to choose from for small and new businesses – the problem is how to locate them. Some grants pop up and are available only for a short time, so before you find them the application date has expired. What you do, where you do it and a number of other factors determine whether or not your business qualifies for grant aided assistance. The uses the grants can be put to are numerous and range from feasibility studies to product development costs and, in some cases, start-up costs.

Many grants are awarded by the government through the Department of Trade and Industry. These can be located through Business Links. Others can be obtained through the European Union, regional development agencies, local councils and county enterprise boards.

At any one time there are over 2,000 grants available throughout the UK and about 600 soft loans. A soft loan is one with little or no interest levied on it. It's impossible to keep track of every one of these, so as well as checking out your nearest Business Link office or website (which usually has over 500 different grants available at any one time), do visit the following websites, which also offer excellent search facilities:

- www.grantsonline.org.uk – this website provides the very latest information on grant funding opportunities ranging from the European Union, UK Government, Regional Grant Making bodies and Grant Making Trusts.

- www.j4bgrants.co.uk – not only does this website have numerous grant facilities on offer, but once you have registered on the site, which is free of charge, you will receive a fortnightly newsletter that will inform you of any new grants that have been launched and remind you of the closing date of others as it nears.

The Small Firms Loan Guarantee (SFLG) scheme is available to small and medium-sized businesses and start-ups and it's a joint venture between the Department of Trade and Industry and a number of approved lenders. So if you have a viable business idea that requires funding, but you are unable to access normal lenders due to a lack of suitable assets to offer as security, then the SFLG helps to overcome this problem by providing lenders with a government guarantee against default.

The cost of this guarantee is currently two per cent of the outstanding balance per year, payable to the Department of Trade and Industry in addition to the normal interest rates charged. The main features of this scheme are as follows:

- The guarantee covers 75 per cent of the loan.

- The borrower pays two per cent per annum additional interest.

- It covers loans of up to £250,000.

- It's available to firms with turnover up to £5.6 million and under five years old.

- Loans are available for most business purposes, but there are some restrictions.

If your application for a business loan is turned down due to insufficient security, ask the lender to submit your application to the Department for Business, Enterprise & Regulatory Reform for consideration under the SFLG scheme.

If using this scheme is the only way to get your business started, then the extra cost will be worth it.

Analysing your business funding

Before approaching any lender, make sure that you have considered every angle and know what financial arrangement is best for your business. When meeting with a potential lender or investor, be confident. Be able to say how much funding you will need, what use it will be put to and how long you will want the funding to last. Armed with this material, a good business idea and a well thought out business strategy, your business should get off the ground in next to no time.

These guidelines also apply to those businesses on the verge of expansion. Think through why you need to expand and the benefits it will bring, not only to you and your current staff, but also to the local community through job creation. Updating your business plan and including new marketing data will also go a long way to convince potential lenders that you have thought through your expansion plans thoroughly.

 Use a combination of lenders and a mix of finance facilities. Borrow what is right for you, not for the lender.

CHAPTER 8

Structuring your business plan

What you'll find in this chapter

✔ Why you need a business plan
✔ Basic ingredients
✔ Constructing your business plan
✔ Practical steps to get you started
✔ Choosing the right name
✔ Business plan digest

By now you should be fully aware of the knowledge and the resources you will need to achieve your ambitions in your chosen field of business. In addition, you probably know which assets you lack, but you will also know where and how to acquire them. Now is the time to put all those facts and figures you have been gathering into a formal report, one which you can use to measure the performance of your business.

You may know precisely what you want to do and how you are going to accomplish your plans, but unless this information is written down and presented in a professional manner, your ideas won't get a second glance.

Outsiders, if they are to consider investing in your business, will demand to see your every move – in precise black and white terms. Your business plan will tell them in minute detail how you will attain sufficient profitable sales to make your efforts worthwhile. Hopefully, your business ideas will develop continually. As they do, write them down. If you can think of the consequences of each step and mould these ideas until they are just right for you, then you will always be ahead of the game. Don't ever think that concepts must be discarded because they proved to be unworkable. As you expand they may be adapted or rethought into profitable notions.

The more homework you do before actually starting your business, the better. You will stand less risk of failure if you don't rush into it prematurely. Once you are confident that your preparation is complete, you can start setting out your stall, by way of a business plan.

 Some people start a business and prosper without any plan at all, but for every firm that does get by without planning, many more fail.

Why you need a business plan

The importance of having a business plan has been continually stated throughout this book, yet it cannot be stressed enough. Think of it as your business's CV, but instead of asserting your achievements, it advertises your ambitions and the solid business methods you will use to attain your goals.

As time goes by, you will be able to see whether the business is performing to expectation. If it's not, you will be able to modify your methods and bring your business back to a profitable route. Bringing all the information together will give you an integrated picture of how your business will work and will help you avoid the many common pitfalls of running a business.

Drawing up your firm's plan will ensure that you have:

- confirmed that the business is viable;
- identified strengths and weaknesses and developed improvements;
- targets by which you can measure your success;
- a coherent picture of your aims and how these will be achieved;
- the opportunity to discover different 'what if' scenarios without risk;
- a presentation document for fund-raising.

A good business model or forecast will allow you to have a clear plan of action for you, your staff and management, as well as providing you with the opportunity to jettison those elements which are impractical, unprofitable or potentially disastrous.

Basic ingredients

All business modules share common characteristics: they cover one-to three-year trading periods, they disclose how your business is expected to perform and include the following:

- The details of your product or service.

- The type of business you are or will be operating.

- An agreed management structure.

- The details of the business's main suppliers and costs.

- Market research and a marketing plan.

- Operational and financial plans.

- The identity of key personnel.

- The details of how the business will develop.

- Quotes for any refurbishment your business premises may require.

- A list of equipment you will need, with costs.

- Three-year cash flow forecasts.

Once you have completed your business plan, you should have answered these four key questions with a degree of confidence:

1. Will people buy my product or service?

2. Can I produce or provide it?

3. Can I make money at it?

4. Can I finance the project?

Now let's see how a business plan should look in order for it to have the maximum effect. A case study and specimen business plan that you can adapt for your own use is to be found at the end of this book.

Constructing your business plan

Apart from the details mentioned in the last segment, the front cover of your plan will identify:

- the name, address, telephone, fax and internet address (if you have one) of your business;

- the period the plan covers;

- capital structure;

- when trading will start or when it began (if you are already trading).

The capital structure shows in brief whose money has been put into the business. Unless the business is up and running, however, it will be the owner(s)'. The wording will depend upon the form your trading will take. A sample of the distinct variations follows:

1. **Sole trader.** If you are trading on your own, give the name of the owner (i.e. yourself) and any trading name you have adopted, plus the amount you are personally investing, and include the value of any equipment you are bringing to the business. For instance:

Owner's name	Capital invested (£)
Penny Sterling	10,000

During this section you may find it helpful to turn intermittently to the case study in the Appendix to see how this data fits in.

2. **Partnership.** Partnership details should be given in the same manner as a sole trader. For example:

Partner's name	Capital invested (£)
Penny Sterling	5,000
Mark Cash	5,000

3. **Limited company.** This differs slightly from the previous two forms of business. Give the name of each person and indicate whether he is a director or shareholder (in a new business he is almost always both), the number and value of ordinary shares he holds and the percentage held. Also, show any loans each individual has made to the business. This is illustrated thus:

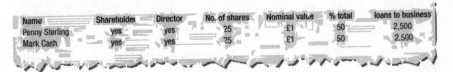

Name	Shareholder	Director	No. of shares	Nominal value	% total	loans to business
Penny Sterling	yes	yes	25	£1	50	2,500
Mark Cash	yes	yes	25	£1	50	2,500

Be sure to include all directors and major shareholders. Instead of a chart, you may prefer to write a brief paragraph on each company member and officer.

4. **Co-operatives (unlimited and limited).** These are more or less the same as a partnership. For an unlimited co-operative the amount invested will be shown as capital invested. For a limited one it will be stated as loans to business.

Member's name	Capital invested (£)
Penny Sterling	5,000
Mark Cash	3,000
Peter Franc	2,000

The different forms of trading mentioned above are covered in greater detail, along with their advantages and disadvantages, in the following chapter.

 When planning your business, ponder every aspect seriously. Then think hard, think long and then think again.

Mission statements

In some circles they are called 'executive summaries' and these are best described as a vision statement. While personal objectives are not normally included in a business plan, there is no reason why they cannot be recorded. The purpose of the statement is to remind you of what you want out of the business. Make sure that your business aims take into account your personal objectives, but beware, sometimes business growth cannot be achieved without sacrificing personal goals.

It's up to you to live up to the vision. You will need to communicate this vision to everyone working for the organisation. The mission statement also needs to convey that you are good at what you do. A typical mission statement might state:

'To provide the best customer service, through well-trained, competent, motivated and happy staff.' Or 'Constantly being the best run garage in Manchester, run by people who care.'

A mission statement sets the scene against which the business objectives can be established. These objectives will give direction and targets to your business. They should also help you to resolve short-term problems. The definition of your business objectives is the most important thing, enabling you to keep track of where you are going and how you will get there!

 Long-term objectives can be achieved by setting a series of short-term targets. The targets should initially be set for a year, then for subsequent years, to help you stay on target.

For the first year of your business plan your business targets need to be set under separate headings, such as:

- **Implementation plan (business objectives):** this is the path you will follow to get your business off the ground during the start-up period and will include how you will introduce health and safety measures and any of the other legal requirements you need to impose to ensure that you meet the licensing requirements explained in chapter 1.

- **Financial:** the main information in this section will be:

  - to obtain a return on investment of 15 per cent before tax;

  - to achieve net profits of £50,000 per annum.

  In addition, it should demonstrate in the form of a cash flow forecast the periods when you will have surplus finances and those times when there might not be enough money coming in, as well as your plans for dealing with this shortfall (e.g. arranging overdraft facilities with your bankers).

- **Marketing:**

  - Reach sales of £80,000 per month.

  - Increase the customer base by five new customers per month.

  This summary will contain details of your marketing plan for the business. This will be based on the information you gathered when you conducted your market research. It should also state the cost of any advertising, details of any public relations articles you are planning, as well as explaining how you will measure the success of each method of marketing you intend using.

- **Operations:**

  - Maintain machine operation at 85 per cent of working time.

  - Produce 20 units per hour at a cost of £9.50 per unit.

  Also, you should include in this part of your business plan an enhancement of the products or services you intend selling and how they fit in with your findings from the market research exercise, if appropriate.

 Don't try to be clever by papering over any cracks in your business plan. If your scheme isn't foolproof, it won't take an experienced financier long to see through it.

Practical steps to get you started

As you go through each stage of your business planning, put all your findings down on paper. You may find that some of the data you have collected is of little or no use to you, but it's always better to have too much information than too little.

It doesn't matter in which order you collect your information. Nevertheless, it's important that the report provides an honest picture of your intentions and ambitions. Moreover, it needs to be submitted in a logical order to avoid any confusion forming in the mind of a possible lender or investor.

In the event that you are unsure of any part of your business plan, seek the advice of an accountant or similar professional before submitting it.

Decide on a trading name and, if possible, select your business premises before writing your business plan, but don't commit to anything until you are sure that you have all the finances in place. If someone else gets your desired premises before you are ready, don't worry; your plan can easily be altered.

Choosing the right name

Selecting the right name for your business will help it stand out from the rest. However, there are a few restrictions that could affect your choice. A sole trader or partnership can trade in their own names. On the other hand, they can opt for a trading name, but they will have to include their own names and addresses on all business stationery.

A limited company must register its name when formed and it cannot use the same name of any other company on the register at Companies House. The name you choose must not be misleading or contain words such as 'royal' or 'institute'. Having 'international' within the title when you run a small corner shop will also be frowned upon.

To check out your intended name to make sure that it's suitable and available, you can do a search at www.companieshouse.gov.uk/info. However, if you are considering setting up a website for your business, it's also advisable to check if the name is available as a web address (domain name). Domain names can be checked very easily at either Nominet at www.nic.uk or Netnames at www.netnames.co.uk.

Now go to the Appendix and see for yourself what a feasible business plan should look like.

> **TIP** A well-designed letterhead and business logo are invaluable to a new business. Go to a little extra expense; it will be worth it!

Business plan digest

Talk to all those who will be involved in your business. Note their ideas and listen closely to any doubts that might be expressed. Present your business plan clearly and precisely. Tell it as it is, warts and all.

Once you have completed your business plan, remember that this is not the end. Business plans are working documents and they need to be read and brought up to date as circumstances dictate.

CHAPTER 9

Tax and other things

What you'll find in this chapter

✔ Preventing money laundering
✔ Insurance
✔ Forms of trading
✔ Help and advice
✔ Time to recollect
✔ Further sources of information

Someone once said, 'only two things are certain in life – death and taxes'. Happily, we shall not be discussing the former in detail. Unfortunately, we do have to mention taxes. You must make provision for tax and insurance. Tax demands have the habit of popping through your letterbox when your cash flow is at its lowest, and they have to be paid no matter what state your finances are in. Likewise, insurance; if a disaster that isn't covered strikes your business, you'll soon be shutting up shop.

 The cost of advice from an accountant or tax specialist could be more than covered by the savings in time and money they recommend.

The Inland Revenue and Customs & Excise have recently joined forces and operate collectively under one banner HM Revenue & Customs. All duties are now paid to this department and all returns can now be completed online. In the different segments that follow relating to taxes and VAT, the current rates can change from time to time, but you can check for the latest rates by logging on to www.hmrc.gov.uk.

Everyone is liable to pay Income Tax and National Insurance, whether a sole trader, a partner or director of a company. These two, together with Corporation and Inheritance Tax, are called 'direct taxation'. If your business turnover exceeds a certain level (check the current level at www.hmrc.gov.uk), VAT must be levied on your goods or services. VAT and stamp duty are classified as indirect taxation. Let's take a glance at the taxes you might have to pay.

- **Income Tax.** Operating as a sole trader means you will pay the normal rates of Income Tax on the whole of your profits, not your level of drawings. If you operate as a partnership, the amount of Income Tax charged to your profits will depend on the Income Tax rates paid by the individual partners on their incomes. Personal allowances are unaffected.

- **National Insurance.** As a self-employed person, you are liable to pay Class 2 National Insurance contributions, unless your earnings are extremely low. Class 4 contributions may also be due if your net profits exceed a specific level (for current levels, see www.hmrc.gov.uk). You will be obliged to deduct National Insurance contributions from the salaries paid to all your employees.

There is a special set of tax and National Insurance rules relating to the construction industry. If your business falls into this category, you are advised to get a copy of 'Construction Industry Scheme (CIS340)' from www.hmrc.gov.uk/leaflets.

The moment you start planning your business, contact the Revenue and Collection Office. You will need to register as self-employed if you are not trading as a limited company. The system for paying your own tax as a self-employed person is called 'self-assessment'. The important feature of self-assessment is that your tax liability is based on your current year of trading, unlike the 'old days' when it was based on your previous 12 months' profits. Other main points include:

- one set of payment dates;
- obligations for keeping records;
- one main point of contact for your tax affairs.

There are fixed, automatic penalties for late returns, and interest and surcharges are payable for late payment. One other major advantage is that you can complete your tax returns online. Full details of self-assessment and current rate of tax and National Insurance contributions for both your staff and yourself can be downloaded from the HM Revenue & Customs' website.

- **VAT (Value Added Tax).** Subject to a minimum threshold, you must register your business for VAT purposes. Not all goods and services are subject to the maximum rate. Some are zero rated, while others are exempt and others have a lower tariff. It's important to be fully aware of the VAT regulation relating to your business.

- **Capital Gains Tax.** This is a tax on capital profits made on items such as investments and land. Capital Gains Tax becomes due if you sell such items for more than you paid for them, after allowing for inflation. Any capital losses arising from the sale of an asset can be offset against any gain within the same tax year.

Using part of your home and charging it to your business could mean Capital Gains Tax might be due when it's sold. Get advice!

- **Inheritance Tax.** This is paid on the value of a deceased estate, at the date of death. This includes property, shares and other personal assets. Any assets transferred to other ownership less than seven years before death are also included. There is a level below which no tax is due. Your accountant will tell you the current figure.

- **Corporation Tax.** This is a tax paid on the profits made by a limited company. Profit is defined as being the total sales less allowable expenses, plus investment income. By increasing allowable expenses the director can reduce the amount of Corporation Tax paid, as well as pension contributions for himself and his staff. Accurate book-keeping records will ensure that your accountant takes into account every expense which can be offset.

There is a range of allowances to which you or your business is entitled. Be careful that you do not pay any more tax than is required.

When deducting tax and National Insurance contributions from employees, there are other payments you must make to an employee, which will be reimbursed from HM Revenue & Customs, for example:

- Family and working tax credits

- Maternity and paternity leave

- Sick pay

In addition, if they have children, you may offer your employees childcare vouchers. This applies to both parents if they are living together. These vouchers, valued at £50 per week, can be used to pay for childcare at a registered provision and have certain tax and National Insurance benefits to both employee and employer. Again, full information can be obtained at the above website.

Preventing money laundering

There are some businesses, and this includes those that accept payment in cash for goods or services that exceed £10,000 (15,000 euros) in a single transaction, which are required to take precautions to prevent money laundering. Those businesses, which must put money laundering procedures in place, include high-value dealers and:

- third-party cheque cashiers;

- bureaux de change and money transmitters;

- estate agents and casinos;

- lawyers and accountants.

All affected businesses need to register with HM Revenue & Customs and pay an annual fee, as well as reporting any changes to their business during the period of registration. Furthermore, employers need to ensure that all staff are fully trained in preventing money laundering, which means:

- verifying the identity of new customers;

- knowing how to identify and report suspicious transactions;

- keeping records of customers and transactions and retaining them for at least five years.

The penalty for failing to register at the correct time could render you liable to a fine of up to £5,000.

Insurance

Protecting your business by having adequate insurance cover not only makes sense, but in some circumstances is also compulsory by law. After all, your business could be the only source of income for you and your dependants. Faced by a sudden claim for damages from a customer, or a situation where your enterprise can no longer function because of a fire, how would your business be revived without the benefits of insurance? Furthermore, customers lost during a time of inactivity may never be recovered. Therefore, it's highly advisable that you consult a reputable insurance broker to make sure that you get the right insurance programme to cover your business.

 Do you know that it's possible to insure against the loss of key staff due to illness?

Compulsory insurance

- **Public liability** will protect you against legal action taken by members of the public (not employees) that arise from your business activities. While this is not really a compulsory item it's placed here, at the top of the list, to stress how vital this cover is.

- **Employers' liability.** If you employ people other than your family, you are legally required to take out employers' liability cover. This protects you against claims from employees that arise from injury or death sustained at work or in the course of their employment.

- **Engineers' plant policies or contracts.** Inspection of certain types of plant and equipment by a competent person is mandatory. Noncompliance could mean a complete shutdown of your operation. An annual inspection contract or policy is required to be in force to comply with these regulations.

- **Motor insurance.** Current legislation specifies that it's compulsory to have third-party liability insurance on all motor vehicles scheduled in the Road Traffic Act. Company vehicles that are an asset of your business need to be covered against material damage by comprehensive cover.

 Private cars used for business purposes, such as taking money to the bank, must not be restricted to social, domestic and pleasure insurance cover.

Non-compulsory insurance

Don't skimp on cover simply because the following types are not compulsory. Remember that it's your assets and livelihood that are at risk.

 The types of insurance shown here are just some of the main types of cover available. Confer with your insurance broker and check on your insurance needs regularly.

- **Material damage insurance.** If you are leasing your business premises, covering the building may be part of the contract. This cover should also protect your stock and equipment against dangers such as fire, flood, storm, burst pipes and other specified causes.

- **Product liability.** This will provide cover for any legal liability arising from claims against you from members of the public for bodily injury or damage to their property from goods supplied, serviced, tested or repaired by you or your staff.

- **Loss of profits.** In the event that your business premises are unusable as a result of an insured peril, a fire for example, the income of the business will be maintained as if the disaster had not occurred.

- **Goods in transit.** Motor vehicle policies don't normally cover goods in a vehicle. This policy would cover goods being delivered to customers either in your own vehicles or sent by any other means.

- **Professional indemnity** offers cover for legal liability for professional errors and omissions made while carrying out your business. It will also cover those working for you.

- **Pensions.** A pension scheme will provide a tax-efficient fund to provide income in retirement, thereby reducing long-term dependency on your business. Some businesses also provide pension schemes for their staff. These are complex issues and any pension you may be considering should not be entered into lightly, nor without the help of a specialist financial adviser.

Details of your current insurance coverage and any other types of insurance you are considering should be noted in your business plan.

 If there is a trade association for the type of business you operate, enquire about any special insurance cover it has negotiated. Premiums may be cheaper.

Forms of trading

Before you commence trading you need to consider the legal form your business will take, although the type of business you will be operating will have some influence on your decision. Each classification has its advantages and disadvantages. The salient points are summarised below:

- **Sole trader.** This is exactly what it sounds like. Someone who owns and runs a business as an individual; the ultimate responsibilities will rest with him. Any profit made belongs to the sole trader. You simply decide to start trading and off you go. You should tell HM Revenue & Customs that you have started trading as a self-employed person.

  There is no need to register a business name, but you cannot trade in the name of somebody who is already trading. Words such as 'royal' and 'institute' require special permission. Read the booklet 'Business Names – Guidance Notes' available free from the Companies Registration Office, Cardiff.

Advantages	Easy to set up
	Few legal implications
	One-person ownership
Disadvantages	If the business fails, you could lose everything you own
	You are personally liable for your employees' actions

- **Partnership.** A number of people who pool their resources and knowledge into a single business in which they are joint owners. When forming a partnership it's worth considering a 'partnership agreement'. This is not a sign of distrust but simply a document setting out who invests what, and how profits are to be shared; not forgetting details of each partner's duties and responsibilities. Every partner is deemed jointly and severally liable. This means that you are responsible both collectively and individually for the business debts, even if they were not incurred by you.

Advantages	Somewhat easy to set up
	Many heads are better than one
	Fewer legal implications than a company
Disadvantages	You are held responsible for your partners' commercial decisions
	You must pay the partners' shares of the business debts if they don't pay

- **Limited liability partnership.** A limited liability partnership shares many of the features of a normal partnership, but it also offers reduced personal responsibility for business debts. The cost of setting up this type of partnership is more expensive and complicated than setting up a normal partnership. A limited partnership vehicle is not generally used these days for running a business, although charities do make good use of them.

- **Limited company.** This legal identity is separate from those who set it up and own the shares. A limited company is owned by its shareholders and directors are appointed to run it. In a small business it's likely that the directors and shareholders are the same people. In a limited company you must issue a minimum of two shares and appoint two directors, one of whom must be the company secretary. The directors of a small company may be husband and wife. A company secretary is responsible for ensuring that all legal obligations are met.

Advantages	Greater opportunity to raise finance
	Liability is limited
	You are not responsible for the company's debts
Disadvantages	More costly to set up and run
	Must disclose details of business and accounts
	Legal requirements to fulfil

 Directors who are fraudulent or allow the company to trade when CAUTION it's insolvent can be personally liable for the company's debts – Insolvency Act 1986.

- **Co-operative.** Again rarely seen, apart from the local co-ops and building societies we all know and love. The advantages and disadvantages of using this form are the same as limited companies and partnerships, with additional drawbacks such as the following:

  - Returns are not based upon the level of financial investment.

  - All members have equal voting rights; rights which are not based on the level of share ownership.

  - Return on money invested is limited.

- **Community Interest Company (CIC).** It's a company established to trade for the good of the community. The legal framework for this new kind of company can be found in the Companies (Audit, Investigation and Community Enterprise) Act 2004 and the Community Interest Company Regulations 2005. The main feature that separates this type of company from any other is the 'asset lock', which means that the assets and profits of the company must be permanently retained and used solely for the benefit of the community.

- **Franchise.** This is becoming an increasingly popular way to start a business. This option allows you to operate a business using an established format. A franchiser grants you the right to use his trade name, product or service and provides back-up support and management skills. In return, you invest time, effort and money. A franchiser has a vested interest in your success, so using this format can be less risky than going it alone. Many of the high-street banks have set up special departments to deal with franchises.

 Care is needed when buying a franchise. Make sure that you investigate it thoroughly. If you believe over-optimistic projections without conducting your own research, you can run the risk of failure.

 Search your local *Yellow Pages* for your area to avoid using a name that clashes with an existing business.

All you need to ask yourself now is, 'What type of business will I be running?'

Help and advice

At first it must seem a frustrating and overwhelming task; putting together a business takes an enormous amount of time and effort. Fortunately, there is always a light at the end of the tunnel. There are people and organisations ready and willing to help and offer advice. All you have to do is ask them to help.

Never put off asking for advice and always seek it sooner rather than later. This will help you to avoid making costly mistakes and stop you from going broke. Apart from the organisations mentioned in various parts of this book, don't forget friends and family. At the end of this chapter you will find a list of useful websites, which are overflowing with help and advice. Use them as often as you need.

There will be times when you will need help from professional advisers, such as accountants and solicitors. They will charge you a fee and they are not cheap. However, most professional advisers usually offer a free preliminary interview. Use this period to assess whether they are the right solicitor or accountant for you. Ask for details of their charges, and again haggle.

Banks are also convenient sources of advice, but they can be biased in relation to the services they offer, so beware. Furthermore, they will charge for providing this service and sometimes their costs are not always clear.

There is also a range of government-backed initiatives aimed at those new to commerce. Although each service has its own area of operation, they do work in partnership with each other. Each of the following three services can be found in your local telephone directory, or contacted through the Department for Business, Enterprise & Regulatory Reform on 020 7215 5000 or at www.berr.gov.uk.

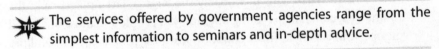

The services offered by government agencies range from the simplest information to seminars and in-depth advice.

- **Local small business centres.** These can help you when you are starting up your business. Such centres, supported by major business organisations, offer impartial and confidential advice without charge. Please note that while some types of business training is offered free of charge, others will charge a small fee. You should contact the small business centre in the area where your business will be located, not in the area where you live.

- **Business Link.** For the established business with ten or more employees, Business Link offers the best package. Its goal is to support firms on the brink of expansion and it achieves this aim by providing each company with a team of business advisers who are specialists either in a particular subject or with knowledge of certain business sectors. Its website address is www.businesslink.gov.uk.

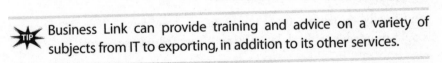

Business Link can provide training and advice on a variety of subjects from IT to exporting, in addition to its other services.

- **National Federation of Enterprise Agencies.** This runs business start-up schemes aimed at the unemployed who wish to start their own business. In certain areas, financial support, grants and loans on special terms may be available. To find out more, telephone 01234 831 623 or visit its website at www.nfea.com.

The following independent organisations can also help:

- **The Forum of Private Business.** This is an independent enterprise offering a platform for the small business community to air their grievances by lobbying the government. Membership also provides a number of other benefits. Telephone 01565 634 467 or visit www.fpb. org for more information.

- **Chambers of Commerce.** These are the national voice of business. They provide a varied range of commercial services with member discounts. For details of your local Chamber, contact the British Chambers of Commerce on 020 7654 5800 (www.chamberonline. co.uk).

- **The Prince's Trust.** This is probably the largest start-up agency in the voluntary sector. It helps young unemployed people and those of limited means. Young people from ethnic minorities, people with disabilities and young ex-offenders are all welcome. Would-be entrepreneurs will need to have a good business idea and be able to demonstrate commitment and enthusiasm. To contact The Prince's Trust, telephone 0800 842 842 or visit its website at www.princes-trust.org.uk.

Time to recollect

A lot of help and advice is obtainable free of charge, so don't be too proud to ask for it. Make time to talk to anybody who can assist you. Constantly refer to the respective chapters of this book if you are unsure where to turn.

To sum up the secrets of starting and running a successful business, it's not having lots of money, but the ability to keep customers satisfied and getting good staff and retaining them.

And finally, remember that entrepreneurs don't have any rules. They are single-minded, can think laterally and treat failure as a learning curve.

Further sources of information

In general, the first point of contact for anyone seeking information is the internet. It's fast and you can download all the information you need immediately. However, sometimes people prefer to talk to someone and telephone requests for information are usually dealt with on the same day. The sources of information printed here may not have been provided elsewhere in this book.

- **Better Payment Practice Group** provides advice on getting paid on time. Contact www.payontime.co.uk.

- **British Standards Institute** supplies itemised information on all British standards, in particular payment standards and BS ISO 9000. Telephone 020 8996 9001 with your enquiries. Website: www.bsi.org.uk.

- **Chartered Institute of Marketing,** for sales, marketing and related information, and details on seminars and recruitment issues. For all enquiries, telephone 01628 427 500. Website: www.cim.co.uk.

- **Companies House** holds records of all limited companies and will provide leaflets on directors' obligations, filing annual returns and accounts. For assistance, telephone 0870 333 3636. Website: www.companies-house.gov.uk.

- **Information Commissioner's Office.** For all data protection registration requirements, call 0845 630 6060. Website: www.ico.gov.uk.

- **Institute of Directors** offers free practical business information for its members. It assists small businesses in all aspects of starting a business. General enquiries can be made by dialling 020 7839 1233. Website: www.iod.co.uk.

- **Office of Fair Trading (Consumer Credit Licensing Branch).** If you are offering non-trade customers any form of consumer finance, you are required to obtain a consumer credit licence. For details, telephone 0845 404 0506. Website: www.oft.gov.uk.

- **UK Intellectual Property Office** for tangible help to protect your designs, trademarks and inventions. Simply telephone 0845 950 0505. Website: www.ipo.gov.uk.

Accounting and credit

- **Association of Chartered Certified Accountants** (www.acca.co.uk)

- **Institute of Chartered Accountants in England and Wales** (www.icaew.co.uk)
- **Institute of Credit Management** (www.icm.org.uk)

Finance

- **Asset Based Finance Association** (www.abfa.org.uk)
- **Finance & Leasing Association** (www.fla.org.uk)

Franchising

- **British Franchise Association** (www.thebfa.org)

Legal

- **Her Majesty's Courts Service** (www.hmcourts-service.gov.uk)
- **Law Society** (www.lawsociety.org.uk offers 30 minutes of free advice for your business)

Research

- **Chartered Institute of Management Accountants** (www.cimaglobal.com)
- **Confederation of British Industry** (www.cbi.org.uk – a priceless source of information)

APPENDIX

Case study and sample business plan

Case study – Sales Ledger Services

Introduction

Mike Cunningham has been employed as a credit manager for the last six years with a trade finance company. Due to a recent merger, he has been offered an attractive redundancy package. Having toyed with the idea of setting up his own business for a couple of years, he thinks this is an opportunity not to be missed.

Using the knowledge he has gained over the preceding years, Mike plans to set up a business as a sole trader by establishing 'Sales Ledger Services' (SLS), a new business service aimed at small to medium-sized firms. He chooses to rent office accommodation in an office complex near to the town centre, which has ample car parking, as well as facilities for his clients and staff. It's convenient to all major road networks, offering easy access to the nearby towns and industrial estates, thus enlarging the catchment area for increasing his client base. Mike decides to prepare his business plan for one year and intends to commence trading on 1 September.

Mission statement and business objectives

Mike believes in using well-trained staff who will be eager to provide a quality service and take extra care of his clients. His primary targets are to establish the business and take drawings of £15,000 in the first year. In this first year, he anticipates making a loss of about £3,000. In the second year, he aims to increase his drawings to £20,000 and produce profits of £30,000.

Capital and personal circumstances

Mike has £5,000 savings, the redundancy payment of £10,000 and a car, valued at another £5,000, which he is putting into the business. He is married with a teenage daughter. Mike's wife doesn't work at present but she's agreed to help out part-time. Her wages are included in the first year's drawings. National Insurance and Income Tax will also be paid from the drawings.

Key employees

In the beginning, apart from Mike and his wife, there will be one full-time employee. He calculates that within two months another full-time and possibly a further two part-time staff will be required. The initial staff will be:

- **Mike Cunningham,** the owner, 40 years of age. A Fellow of the Institute of Credit Management, he has worked as an accounts clerk, a credit controller, a supervisor covering all aspects of credit control and in management. In the past he has worked for manufacturing and service industries, in medium and large firms. Mike's knowledge and experience includes both manual and computer sales ledger accounting systems.

- **Linda Cunningham,** aged 34 years old. Linda hasn't worked since their daughter was born, but she is a trained book-keeper and is arranging to go on a refresher course, which also covers computerised accounting.

- **Karen Swift,** a credit control supervisor, is 28 years old. Karen spent a number of years as an accounts clerk with a leasing company before leaving to work with Mike as a credit control trainee. Quickly promoted, they worked as a team, reducing the level of outstanding debt. Unhappy with her new employers she plans to join Mike in this endeavour.

Marketing

Sales Ledger Services plans to operate initially within a 25-mile radius of its offices, with information supplied by the local Business Link. Mike discovers that there are nearly 3,750 small businesses in his area. In addition, about 1,400 start up every quarter and about 1,200 close within that period. The main reason given for the closures were inadequate financial controls. He hopes that his service will mean fewer closures for these businesses.

Mike conducts market research by post and telephone. He purchases a mailing list comprising small and medium-sized businesses from the local Business Link and targets firms with fewer than 20 employees in the manufacturing and service sectors. The information he obtains supplies him with enough data to confirm that his idea is viable.

Mike also compiles a questionnaire and sends it, along with a reply-paid envelope and covering letter, explaining the service he proposes, to 200 prospective clients. He uses the same questionnaire to telephone a further 100 businesspeople. Within the body of the questionnaire he asks:

Does your company offer trade credit?

For what period – 30, 60, 90 days or longer?

Do customers exceed their credit terms?

If your customers paid earlier, would this benefit your business?

Therefore, would you be interested in further details of this service?

When would be the best day and time to contact you?

Is there a similar service you would like to be offered?

He makes clear that only those who indicate their interest by responding to the questionnaire will be bothered again. The covering letter and telephone call are both finished by thanking the people for their time.

Mike discovers from the telephone research that 14 per cent request further details of his service, eight per cent state that they would be interested in a book-keeping service and five per cent suggest a payroll service. A further two per cent request details of all three services.

The response to the postal survey is not as impressive. Only 48 per cent reply, and of these, only nine per cent require more details. Another four per cent suggest the payroll services and one per cent the book-keeping services. No one requests all three.

From this research, Mike knows that he has a possible 40 clients for his sales ledger service, but by adding book-keeping and payroll to his services, a further 20 possible clients can be added. Mike hopes that these customers may be persuaded to use his other services later on and realises that by introducing these other services, the success of his business will not be reliant upon just one service.

Another thing Mike learns through his research is that word of mouth is clearly the best way to promote a business. Until the business is established, Mike will have to rely on direct mailing, telephone and personal calling. He hopes that his local paper might carry an article on his new venture in its business pages. A promotional budget of £4,000 has been allocated.

His major competitors for the sales ledger service are book-keeping services, payroll agencies and factoring companies. While the factoring competitors will have the advantage of offering clients cash for their invoices, Mike feels that the personal service and system of credit control he offers will improve his client customers' payment habits. Therefore, the need for supplying his clients with upfront cash will be eliminated. In fact, smaller firms prefer Mike's personal onsite service; they feel more comfortable with their sales ledger operation being kept in-house. Mike also faces competition from other book-keeping and payroll agencies, as well as accounting practices, but his prime service gives him the edge over his rivals.

Premises

Unsure of the size of the office accommodation he will eventually require, Mike agrees to rent a 500-square-foot office in a seedbed centre. This has the added advantage of having some small business clients close by. The rent is agreed for the first six months, but must be renegotiated on a monthly basis thereafter. This allows Mike to expand his business without having to move location. Being newly-built premises and with carpets included, little fitting out is required, except for desks, chairs and any furniture required for a small reception area.

Materials

Apart from a continuing supply of advertising brochures, letterheadings, invoices and business cards, no other supplies are envisaged.

Staffing

Mike and Karen are the two 'full-time' employees. However, to deal with the immediate staffing needs, Mike must recruit two part-time employees straight away – an experienced book-keeper and a payroll clerk. In the meantime, Linda will breach the gap.

Equipment

A telephone and fax are installed. Desks, filing cabinets, chairs, etc. will be purchased at auction. £2,000 has been set aside for good quality furniture. Two desktop computers are a necessity, together with two laptops, so Mike decides to lease these items at £160 per month. The sales ledger software will be purchased 'off the shelf' and modified. Standard book-keeping and payroll systems will be used.

Transport

Mike's car is transferred to the business and the running costs are paid by the business. An adjustment will be made to his Income Tax because of the benefit he will enjoy. Mike decides to employ only those people who have access to a motor vehicle. As Karen and any of these new staff members will need to use their cars for business, a mileage allowance of 40p per mile will be paid.

Insurance

The staff are expected to modify their own motor insurance. Property insurance for the office is included in the rent. Mike takes out a contents policy, as well as obtaining public and employers' liability cover. Loss of profit and professional indemnity are also considered a must. Through his insurance broker he arranges for the £2,400 premiums which will cover his car to be paid monthly.

Other costs (all bills and payments include VAT)

Rent and rates	£250 per month
Postage	£600 per year
Telephone	£900 per annum paid quarterly in arrears. The first bill is due in December
Power (heat and light)	£600 per annum paid quarterly in arrears. First account is due in December
Printing and stationery	£4,000 per annum

Depreciation on the car and equipment will be 25 per cent of the reducing balance.

This business plan has been prepared for

Mike Cunningham t/a

SALES LEDGER SERVICES

FOR THE PERIOD

September 2008 to August 2009

Sample business plan (continued)

MISSION STATEMENT

To provide small and medium-sized businesses considered too small to have their own credit departments with a full in-house credit control and sales ledger operation. To reduce clients' sales ledger debts and improve customer service, thereby freeing cash tied up needlessly within their sales ledgers.

BUSINESS OBJECTIVES

1. To commence trading in September 2008. To achieve a drawing of £15,000 per annum in the first year of trading and to break even.

2. To have a customer base of 120 by the end of the first year's trading.

3. To achieve drawing and profits of £50,000 in year two.

4. To maintain a continuing professional training policy.

5. To qualify for an 'Investors in People' award as soon as possible.

6. To provide the best sales ledger, book-keeping and payroll service in the area, both on and off clients' premises.

7. To treat staff in a fair and equitable manner.

8. To resolve any customer query in the shortest time possible.

9. To make Sales Ledger Services a happy place to work at.

10. To ensure that all health and safety and other regulatory obligations are in place prior to opening.

CAPITAL INJECTION

Owner's Name	Capital Invested
Mike Cunningham	£20,000

Made up of £15,000 cash, plus car valued at £5,000.

Sample business plan (continued)

KEY PERSONNEL

Name:	**Mike Cunningham**
Position:	Owner
Qualifications:	Institute of Credit Management Parts I, II and III
Main responsibilities:	Set up, market and manage business. Train staff in credit and sales ledger activities.
Experience:	Nine years' experience in credit and risk management. Credit Manager for P&P Commercial Finance Ltd. Three years at Interim Management, installing credit control systems.
Name:	**Karen Swift**
Position:	Office Manager
Qualifications:	Institute of Credit Management Parts I and II
Main responsibilities:	Support Mike in running business. Set up client computerised sales ledgers. Attend to customers' problems in person and on the telephone. Assist with recruitment and training.
Experience:	Three years' credit control experience, of which two years was spent at supervisory level at P&P Commercial Finance Ltd. Prior to the previous appointment, four years of general accountancy experience was gained with HP Finance Ltd.

Sample business plan (continued)

Name:	**Linda Cunningham**
Position:	Part-time book-keeper
Qualifications:	IAB Diploma in book-keeping
Main responsibilities:	Maintain accounting recorders. Provide book-keeping service for clients.
Experience:	No recent experience.

MARKET REPORT

Market Trends

Within the area of initial operation there is a growing tendency to outsource specialised areas of operation. Areas such as book-keeping, payroll, mailings and cleaning.

At the present time, no one in the targeted area is offering a sales ledger service, apart from the major factoring houses. Generally, these factors are members of the Factors and Discounters Association and usually seek clients with minimum sales of £1 million.

There are no seasonal fluctuations.

In the first year, new clients will increase from 26 to 312. There are no restrictions on expanding the area of operations, once additional resources have been put in place.

Average client profile:

Turnover:	£250,000
Staff:	10
Days sales outstanding:	78

Sources of information were from market research and experience gained working for P&P Commercial Finance Ltd.

'Days sales outstanding' means the average time it takes a customer to pay an invoice when the terms of trade are stated as 30 days.

PRICING POLICY

Unit costs are based on the following parameters, using the average customer profile:

Sales Ledger Services

One unit = two hours' sales ledger and collections work in-house. Charged at £17.50 per hour. An average client will require two units per month. Therefore, unit costs are £35.00 each.

Book-Keeping Services

One unit = an average of seven hours' book-keeping per month. Charged at £12 per hour, the average client will need one unit per month. Consequently, a unit cost of £84.00 each.

Payroll Services

One unit = maintaining a monthly wages bill for up to ten staff. Charged at £12 per hour. Cost per unit is £47.25.

MARKETING PLAN

Target Market

Small to medium-sized firms with fewer than 20 employees.

Method of Promotion

Direct mailing, telephone and person contact. It is hoped to address trade association meetings and talk at Business Link seminars.

Sales Summary (1st Year)

Total fee income: £142,000. Gross promotional expenses: £4,000.

OPERATIONS PLAN

Premises

Sales Ledger Services will operate from:

Sample business plan (continued)

Suite 9, The Seedbed Centre,
Nonsuch Road, Anytown,
Anywhere, ZX12 5YW.

Location

The premises are located on the edge of a busy market town, close to London, situated adjacent to a major road network offering easy access to nearby towns and industrial estates. A mainline station is within walking distance. There is ample car parking facilities for clients and staff.

Tenure

The premises will be held primarily on a six-month agreement, then monthly thereafter. Rent, which includes rates, and premises insurance amounts to £250 per month payable in advance. A deposit of one month's rent is also required. Signwriting at a cost of £150 is needed. Fitting out a small reception area will cost £600. Telephone and fax lines and machines are already installed.

MATERIALS

A continuing supply of brochures, letterheadings, invoices, statements will be required. The first year's costs are estimated at £4,000.

Suppliers

Many printers and stationers are within close proximity, each offering a 24-hour service.

EMPLOYEES

Initial staffing levels will be:	Full-time	2
	Part-time	1
Staffing levels at end of period:	Full-time	6
	Part-time	5

Attendance Requirements

All staff must be prepared to work at our own offices, and on clients' premises.

TRAINING

Linda Cunningham

Booking-keeping and business administration

Duration:	Four days
Trainer:	Business Link
Location:	Small Business Centre
Cost:	Free of charge

Mike Cunningham and Karen Swift

Software and system training

Duration:	Three two-hour sessions
Trainer:	Software and systems provider
Location:	Sales Ledger Services' offices
Cost:	£300

New employees will be trained in software systems at Software Suppliers' offices for a half day. On the job training of Sales Ledger Services' credit control procedures will be ongoing.

EQUIPMENT

Six desks, eight chairs and three filing cabinets will be purchased at auction.

A reception unit is being purpose made. The total cost of these items is £2,000.

Two desktop computers and two laptops will be leased at a rental of £160 per month, payable by direct debit.

TRANSPORT

Transportation is fairly important to the business, as it is expected that some clients will be situated on industrial estates, away from public transport. Getting between clients' premises in the shortest possible time is also important.

Mike's personal car has been transferred to the business and will be used for business and private use. Staff will be required to use their own vehicles for which a mileage allowance of 40p per mile will be paid.

INSURANCE

A combined contents policy for the office equipment has been taken out. This will also include the laptop computers, which will accompany staff when visiting clients' premises. Professional, public and employers' liability are also included. The annual premiums of £2,400 are being paid monthly by direct debit.

Employees are to ensure that their own vehicle insurance offers suitable cover for using the car to visit clients.

OBSERVATIONS

Cash Flow Forecast

You will note in the forecast illustrated that there will be a need for additional short-term funding of £7,000 in the first year.

Therefore, an interest charge will need to be incorporated within this chart.

Profit and Loss Forecast

The interest element from the loan will also need to be incorporated within this prediction.

A calculation for depreciation is omitted from this forecast due to lack of space. The annual charge for depreciation for Mike's car and office furniture will amount to £1,750 per annum. Computed at 25 per cent of cost.

Mission Statement

Mike's business objectives for the second year will be on track if the forecasts continue into 2009.

Sample business plan (continued)

SALES LEDGER SERVICES
CASH FLOW FORECAST Sept 2008 to August 2009

Month	Sept £	Oct £	Nov £	Dec £	Jan £	Feb £	Mar £	Apr £	May £	Jun £	July £	Aug £	Total £
RECEIPTS													
Total sales	1,813	3,626	5,439	7,252	9,065	10,878	13,251	14,504	16,317	18,130	19,943	21,756	141,974
Cash invested	15,000												15,000
TOTAL RECEIPTS	16,813	3,626	5,439	7,252	9,065	10,878	13,251	14,504	16,317	18,130	19,943	21,756	156,974
PAYMENTS													
Rent/Rates	250	250	250	250	250	250	250	250	250	250	250	250	3,000
Wages	5,000	5,000	7,650	7,650	7,650	10,350	10,350	10,350	10,350	14,000	14,000	15,950	118,300
Printing	2,500				250	250	250	250			250	250	4,000
Telephone		225			225			225				225	900
Light/Heating		150			150			150				150	600
Insurance	200	200	200	200	200	200	200	200	200	200	200	200	2,400
Lease Rentals	160	160	160	160	320	320	320	320	480	480	480	480	3,840
Transport	60	60	80	70	110	110	120	120	140	140	160	180	1,350
Postage	50	50	50	25	75	50	50	50	50	50	50	50	600
Training	300				300		150			150			900
Drawings	1,250	1,250	1,250	1,250	1,250	1,250	1,250	1,250	1,250	1,250	1,250	1,250	15,000
TOTAL PAYMENTS	9,770	7,345	9,640	9,605	10,780	12,780	12,940	13,165	12,720	16,520	16,640	18,985	150,890
NET CASH FLOW	7,043	-3,719	-4,201	-2,353	-1,715	-1,902	311	1,339	3,597	1,610	3,303	2,771	6,084
CUM. CASH FLOW	7,043	3,324	-877	-3,230	-4,945	-6,847	-6,536	-5,197	-1,600	10	3,313	6,084	

Sample business plan (continued)

SALES LEDGER SERVICES

PROFIT AND LOSS FORECAST Sept 2008 to August 2009

Month	Sept £	Oct £	Nov £	Dec £	Jan £	Feb £	Mar £	Apr £	May £	Jun £	July £	Aug £	Total £
INCOME													
Total Sales	1,813	3,626	5,439	7,252	9,065	10,878	13,251	14,504	16,317	18,130	19,943	21,756	141,974
EXPENDITURE (Variable Costs)													
Salaries	3,000	3,000	5,650	5,650	5,650	8,350	8,350	8,350	8,350	12,000	12,000	13,950	94,300
Gross Profit	–1,187	626	–211	1,602	3,415	2,528	4,901	6,154	7,967	6,130	7,943	7,806	47,674
Fixed Costs													
Rent/Rates	250	250	250	250	250	250	250	250	250	250	250	250	3,000
Wages	2,000	2,000	2,000	2,000	2,000	2,000	2,000	2,000	2,000	2,000	2,000	2,000	24,000
Printing	370	330	330	330	330	330	330	330	330	330	330	330	4,000
Telephone	75	75	75	75	75	75	75	75	75	75	75	75	900
Light/Heating	50	50	50	50	50	50	50	50	50	50	50	50	600
Insurance	200	200	200	200	200	200	200	200	200	200	200	200	2,400
Lease Rentals	160	160	160	160	320	320	320	320	480	480	480	480	3,840
Transport	60	60	80	70	110	110	120	120	140	140	160	180	1,350
Postage	50	50	50	50	50	50	50	50	50	50	50	50	600
Training	75	75	75	75	75	75	75	75	75	75	75	75	900
Drawings	1,250	1,250	1,250	1,250	1,250	1,250	1,250	1,250	1,250	1,250	1,250	1,250	15,000
TOTAL FIXED COSTS	4,540	4,500	4,520	4,510	4,710	4,710	4,720	4,720	4,900	4,900	4,920	4,940	56,590
Total Costs	7,540	7,500	10,170	10,160	10,360	13,060	13,070	13,070	13,250	16,900	16,920	18,890	150,890
Net Profit/Loss	–5,727	–3,874	–4,731	–2,908	–1,295	–2,182	181	1,434	3,067	1,230	3,023	2,866	–8,916

Sample business plan (continued)

SALES LEDGER SERVICES
MARKETING FORECAST Sept 2008 to August 2009

Product/Service	Unit Price
Sales Ledger Service	£35.00
Book-Keeping Service	£84.00
Payroll Service	£47.25

Month		Sept	Oct	Nov	Dec	Jan	Feb	Mar	Apr	May	Jun	July	Aug	Total
PRODUCT/SERVICE														
Sales Ledger	Units	32	64	96	128	160	192	240	256	288	320	352	384	2,512
	£	1,120	2,240	3,360	4,480	5,600	6,720	8,400	8,960	10,080	11,200	12,320	13,440	87,920
	Cumulative	1,120	3,360	6,720	11,200	16,800	23,520	31,920	40,880	50,960	62,160	74,480	87,920	
Book-Keeping	Units	6	12	18	24	30	36	42	48	54	60	66	72	468
	£	504	1,008	1,512	2,016	2,520	3,024	3,528	4,032	4,536	5,040	5,544	6,048	39,312
	Cumulative	504	1,512	3,024	5,040	7,560	10,584	14,112	18,144	22,680	27,720	33,264	39,312	
Payroll	Units	4	8	12	16	20	24	28	32	36	40	44	48	312
	£	189	378	567	756	945	1,134	1,323	1,512	1,701	1,890	2,079	2,268	14,742
	Cumulative	189	567	1,134	1,890	2,835	3,969	5,292	6,804	8,505	10,395	12,474	14,742	
Total Monthly Sales		£1,813	3,626	5,439	7,252	9,065	10,878	13,251	14,504	16,317	18,130	19,943	21,756	141,974
Total Cumulative Sales		£1,813	5,439	10,878	18,130	27,195	38,073	51,324	65,828	82,145	100,275	120,218	141,974	
PROMOTIONAL EXPENSES														
Sales Ledger		400	400	400		300	300	300	300	300	300	300	300	3,600
Book-Keeping		50	25	25		25	25	25	25	25	25	25	25	300
Payroll		50	25	25		25	25	25	25	25	25	25	25	300
Total Monthly Promotion		£500	450	450		350	350	350	350	350	350	350	350	4,200
Total Cumulative Promotion		£500	950	1,400		1,750	2,100	2,450	2,800	3,150	3,500	3,850	4,200	

Index

M